SCIENCE FOR BEGINNERS

Contents

Quiz pages by Karen Bryant-Mole

Cover design by Russell Punter

About this book

Science for Beginners aims to challenge and entertain children, but above all, it is intended to make them want to find out more about why things happen in the world around them. Clear, simple explanations of basic concepts are given throughout the book, but no attempt has been made to explain everything, as explanations of some of the more complex principles of science might confuse rather than help young readers. At the end of the first two sections is a glossary where readers can look up the meaning of words that are new to them. Also, at the end of each section is a quiz for children to see how much they can remember.

First published in 1991, Usborne Publishing Ltd, Usborne House, 83-85 Saffron Hill, London EC1N 8RT, England.
Copyright © 1991, 1983 Usborne Publishing Ltd.

The name of Usborne and the device ❦ are trademarks of Usborne Publishing Ltd.

Printed in Great Britain.

SIMPLE SCIENCE

Angela Wilkes
Illustrated by David Mostyn
Consultant: Alan Ward

Contents

Science is all around you

Have you ever looked around you and stopped to wonder why things happen the way they do?

Being a scientist

You can be a scientist and find out things for yourself. This book is full of interesting experiments you can do at home.

How to be a good scientist

Look out for unusual things about everyday objects. Ask yourself what is odd about them and try to think of an answer.

Test your answers with careful experiments. Do each experiment more than once, to check that the same thing happens every time.

Science Notebook

Keep a science notebook. Write down all your experiments in it, step by step, saying what you did and what happened.

Watch carefully when you do experiments. Draw what happens in your science notebook, so you have a record of your results. If an experiment does not seem to work the first time you do it, try doing it again in a different way.

Don't worry if there are things you don't understand straight away. Even famous scientists do not understand everything. There are always new mysteries to solve and new experiments to try.

Air is real

Air is everywhere. It is all around you but you cannot see it. Even things that look as if they are empty are really full of air. The only time you can feel it is when a wind or breeze blows, or when you breathe in and out.

Here are some things to do to show you that air is real, and to help you find out more about it.

Hold a polythene bag open, pull it through the air to trap some air in it, then close it. You cannot see the air in the bag but you can feel how firm and squashy it is.

Now put bits of tissue paper on the floor and drop a book on them. The bits of paper blow away because the falling book pushes air out of the way and makes a wi

The wind

Wind is moving air. Look for signs of movement in this picture. How many things can you see which show that it is a windy day? Do you think there is a gentle breeze or a strong wind blowing? Which direction do you think it is coming from? What would change if the wind stopped blowing?

The wind at work

People use the wind's force to make things move or work. The wind fills the sails of boats and makes them move along and it drives windmills' sails round.

Air not only has the strength to move things; it also slows down things that move through it. Try these experiments to find out how air can slow things down.

Wave a sheet of cardboard up and down. You will feel how the air pushes against it. Wave a bigger sheet of cardboard up and down. Do you notice a difference?

Stand on a chair and try to drop playing cards into a bowl on the floor. Drop some cards end on, and others face down. Which cards usually land in the bowl?

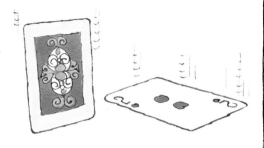

The red card acts like a glider and swoops to one side, but the air pushing up beneath the white card escapes fairly evenly all around it, so it falls straight down.

Why does a parachute come down slowly?

A parachute works in the same way as the card which you dropped face down. As the parachute falls, air is trapped under its canopy and pushes up against it. This makes the parachute fall to the ground slowly and land gently.

Make paper parachutes of your own like the one below. You can test them by dropping them from the top of the stairs, or stand on a chair to drop them.

Paper Parachute

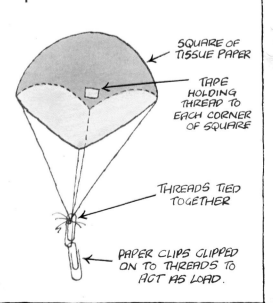

SQUARE OF TISSUE PAPER

TAPE HOLDING THREAD TO EACH CORNER OF SQUARE

THREADS TIED TOGETHER

PAPER CLIPS CLIPPED ON TO THREADS TO ACT AS LOAD.

Parachute tests

Test 1
Clip the same number of paper clips to a big parachute and a smaller one. Which parachute falls more slowly?

Test 2
Test two parachutes the same size but load one of them with more paper clips. What happens?

Test 3
Make a small hole in the top of a parachute and test it again. The hole allows the air trapped under the canopy to escape more smoothly, so the parachute wobbles less.

What happens to warm air?

Blow up a balloon. As you blow, the balloon's skin stretches and swells until the balloon is full of air and feels hard. If you blow any more air into it, it will burst.

Put the balloon in a very warm place, such as an airing cupboard. Leave it there for a few hours, then look at it. Why has the balloon burst?

Why the balloon bursts

The balloon bursts because the air inside it gets bigger and takes up more space as it gets warmer. Scientists say it expands. Air always expands when it is heated.

Hot air rises

Draw a snake like this on a piece of paper and cut it out. Hang it on a thread and hold it above your head. Blow gently up at it and the snake will spin round slowly.

If you hold the snake above a radiator it spins round again. What do you think is making it spin?

What happens

When you blow up at the snake, your breath makes it spin round. When you hold it above a radiator it spins round because hot air is rising from the radiator. When air is heated, it expands, becomes lighter than the cold air round it and rises.

Hot air balloons

Hot air balloons have hot air inside them. This makes them lighter than the cold air around them, so they rise off the ground.

A gas burner heats the air inside the balloon. The pilot can control the height of the balloon by turning the gas burner on or off. The balloon goes where the wind blows it.

When the pilot wants to land, he turns the gas burner off. The air inside the balloon cools down and becomes heavier and the balloon comes down to land.

Cooling down and keeping warm

Hot things cool down and cold things warm up until they reach the same temperature as their surroundings. If you leave a hot drink standing for long it tastes cold. Do this test to find out what makes hot water cool down.

Fill three bowls the same size with hot water. Put one bowl outside and the other two indoors. Blow on the water in one of the indoor bowls. Test the temperature of each bowl of water by dipping a finger into it

once a minute. Which bowl of water cools down the most and which one cools down fastest?

Can you keep water warm? Fill two squeezy bottles with hot water and wrap one bottle in cotton wool. Which bottle of water cools down first?

Hot water cools down until it is the same temperature as the air around it. The colder the air, the more the water cools down. It cools down faster if you blow on it, or if it is standing in a breeze.

In the second test the cotton wool round bottle B acts like a blanket. It traps air round the bottle and this helps to stop the heat from escaping so fast.

Trapped air keeps things warm

The pictures here show some of the ways in which trapped air can help to keep things warm.

Birds fluff up their feathers in winter to trap air and keep warm.

The air trapped in and between clothes helps keep us warm.

Wool feels warm because it traps a lot of air in its fibres.

Why do you think pipes are wrapped in soft material?

Bath water stays warmer if it has foam on top of it because air is trapped in the bubbles.

Duvets are light, but feel warm because there is a lot of air trapped between the feathers in them.

Vanishing water

Puddle test

You can record how a puddle dries up. It is best to do it on a warm and sunny day. Find a puddle on a pavement or in the playground and draw a chalk line round it.

Draw around the puddle again every hour and you can chart how fast it dries up. Try doing it again on a cool, cloudy day. Does it make any difference?

Jars of water

Find two jars the same shape and size. Fasten a strip of paper to one of them (A), as shown. Pour two cupfuls of water into each jar and screw a lid tightly on to jar B.

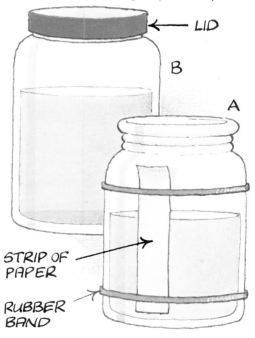

LID

STRIP OF PAPER

RUBBER BAND

Put the jars together on a window-sill and leave them there for a few days. Mark the level of the water on jar A every day. What happens to the level of the water in jar B?

Water does not really disappear when it dries up. Tiny droplets of water rise into the air, but they are so small that you cannot see them and it looks as if the water has vanished. It has turned into water vapour. We say it has evaporated. The air is full of water vapour because water evaporates from oceans, rivers and lakes all the time.

Washing day

How and when is it best for Mrs Bloggs to dry her washing?
On a cold day or a hot day?
On a wet day or a dry day?
On a windy day or a still day?
By folding the clothes or by hanging them up?

Do this test to find out

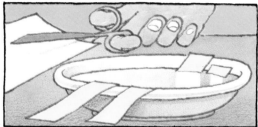

Find a bit of material, cut out six strips all the same size and wet them in a bowl of water.

Put one strip in the sun and.one in the shade.

Hang one in a windy place and one in a still place.

Screw one strip up in a bundle and lay another out flat.

Which strips of material dry the fastest?

Water evaporates fastest in warm, dry places. Washing dries quickly on dry, sunny days and even faster if it is windy too. People hang clothes up because they dry faster if spread out.

Do you ever wonder why you feel cold when you come out of a swimming pool? Because you are wet, the water takes heat from your body as it evaporates.

Evaporating water always cools things down. When your body gets hot, it sweats and the sweat evaporates. This is your body's way of cooling itself down.

Athletes always put on warm clothes after competing. Even if they feel hot, they have sweated a lot and might catch a chill if they did not put on clothes.

Water from air

The water vapour in the air does not always stay there, but can turn back into water again. You can make water appear from nowhere. Put a glass of water in the fridge until it is cold. When you take it out, drops of water appear on the outside of the glass. Where do they come from?

The cold glass cools the air around it. Cold air cannot hold as much water as warm air, so the water vapour in it forms drops of water. This is called condensation.

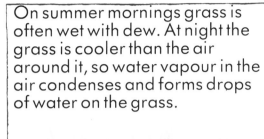

On summer mornings grass is often wet with dew. At night the grass is cooler than the air around it, so water vapour in the air condenses and forms drops of water on the grass.

On winter mornings grass may be covered with frost. Frost is frozen dew. It forms when damp air flows across things that are below freezing temperature.

If you hold a mirror in front of you and blow on it you will see a misty patch made out of lots of tiny drops of water.

There is water vapour in your breath. As your warm, damp breath hits the cold mirror, the water vapour in it condenses.

On a very cold day your breath looks like smoke because the water vapour in it condenses in the air.

What is steam?

DO NOT PUT YOUR FINGER IN THE STEAM!

The same thing happens when steam comes out of a kettle. Water vapour coming out of the kettle cools down as it meets colder air. The droplets of water get bigger and you see steam.

The scientist in the bathroom

WHERE HAVE THESE DROPS OF WATER COME FROM?

WHY IS THE MIRROR MISTY?

WHY IS THERE STEAM IN HERE?

WHAT IS HAPPENING TO THE WATER IN THE BATHROOM?

Where does rain come from?

The water that falls as rain does not just come out of the sky. It comes from the water around us.

The heat of the sun makes water evaporate from the sea and rivers all the time. The warm water vapour rises into the sky.

When it reaches the cold air above the Earth, it condenses into tiny drops of water which join together to form clouds.

The clouds get bigger with more water vapour. Drops of water join together, become heavier and fall to the ground as rain.

Fog is cloud close to the ground. It forms when the air is damp and the ground is cold.

If it is very cold it may snow. The water vapour in the clouds freezes into crystals and these join together to make snowflakes.

Strange effects with water

Water is a liquid and all liquids are fluid. This means that they have no shape of their own but move around easily and take the shape of whatever they are in, whether it is a pipe, a bowl, a bottle or a swimming pool. Unless liquids are put in a container, they spread ou and run away. What do you notice about the direction in which they run?

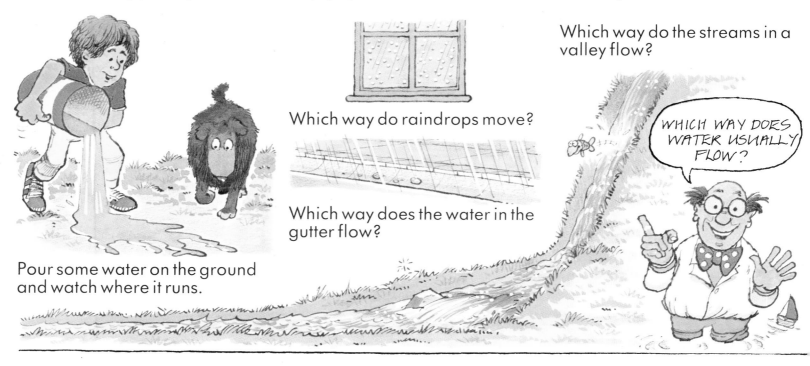

Which way do raindrops move?

Which way does the water in the gutter flow?

Pour some water on the ground and watch where it runs.

Which way do the streams in a valley flow?

WHICH WAY DOES WATER USUALLY FLOW?

Finding out about water levels

Find different shaped transparent containers and half fill each one with water. Draw a line on each container with a felt-tip pen to show where the water level is. Tilt each container in turn and draw the water level again. What happens to the water levels?

THESE EXPERIMENTS SHOW THAT WATER ALWAYS FINDS ITS OWN LEVEL

Do this test above a sink. You need a piece of plastic tubing and a jar of water. Suck some water into the tube and quickly put your finger over the free end.

Now hold the tube up like this and take your finger off the end. Move first one and then the other end of the tube up and down. What happens to the water level?

A magic trick

Suck some water up into a tube, quickly put your finger over the mouth end of the tube and lift the tube up, keeping it upright. All the water will stay in it.

But if you take your finger off the end of the tube, the water pours out of the other end. As air rushes in at one end, the water pours out of the other end.

Making a simple siphon

Fill a jam jar with water and stand it at the edge of a sink. Stand an empty jar in the sink itself so it is lower than the first jam jar.

Suck water up into a tube from the full jar until the tube is full, then quickly put your finger over the mouth end of the tube and put it in the empty jar. Take your finger off the end of the tube.

The water from the full jar will flow into the empty jar. When you remove your finger, water begins to flow out of the bottom end of the tube, but as the other end is in water no air can flow into it, so water flows in instead.

If you lift the bottom jar up above the top one while the tube is still full of water, the water will flow back the other way.

What happened?

Farmer Fred filled his horse's trough with a hosepipe from the nearest tap. When the trough was full he turned off the tap and unhooked the hose, but he left the other end of the hosepipe in the trough. What do you think happened?

The hosepipe acted like a siphon and all the water drained out of the trough.

15

Does water have a skin?

Do these experiments to find out something interesting about the surface of water.

A needle usually sinks if you drop it into water but it is possible to make one float on the surface of the water.

Fill a glass with water. Put a needle on a small piece of tissue and lay it gently on the water. The tissue will sink, but the needle will stay where it is.

Look closely at the surface of the water and you will see that it is dented all round the needle. It is as if the water has a kind of skin and the needle is resting on it.

Surface tension

The needle experiment shows that the surface of water is stronger than it looks and can support things. This strength is called 'surface tension'.

You can sometimes see insects called pond-skaters skimming over the surface of a pond. They can actually walk on water because its 'skin', or surface tension, is strong enough to support them.

Bulging water

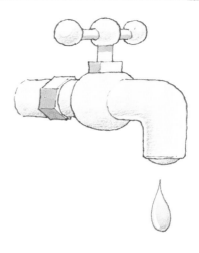

Now try this experiment. Fill a cup to the very top with water, then gently add a bit more, so that the water rises, but does not spill over the edge of the cup.

The water looks as if it is about to overflow, but it does not. Its surface tension is strong enough to hold it in place and stop it from overflowing.

Watch how water drips from a tap and look at the shape of the water drops. The water's 'skin' holds the drops together and gives them their special shape.

Is it magic?

Suck some water up into a straw and put your finger on the mouth-end to hold the water in. Then release some drops of water on to a clean plastic tablecloth.

Look at the shape of the drops of water. Now dip one end of a matchstick into some washing-up liquid and touch each drop of water. What happens to them?

What happens

The surface tension of the water makes the drops of water stand up like buns. When you add washing-up liquid to the water, the drops spread out. This is because the washing-up liquid makes the surface of the water stretchier.

Blowing bubbles

When you blow bubbles, water really does look as if it has a skin and you can see how stretchy it can be.

Make a bubble mixture by stirring washing-up liquid into a cup of water. The washing-up liquid makes the water's 'skin' stretchier, so you can blow better bubbles.

Make a loop out of a bit of thin wire and dip it into the bubble mixture. You will see a thin film of liquid stretched across the loop. Now start blowing bubbles.

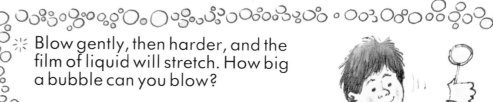

Blow gently, then harder, and the film of liquid will stretch. How big a bubble can you blow?

Are bubbles always the same shape?

Do bubbles change shape when they touch something?

Do bubbles bounce?

When do bubbles pop?

Do bubbles always float downwards?

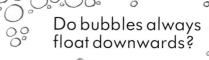

Try blowing a stream of bubbles.

Floaters and sinkers

WHY DOES A BIG IRON SHIP FLOAT?

Next time you get into a bath, watch the level of the water and you will see that it rises. Try this simple experiment to find out what is happening.

Testing for floaters and sinkers

Collect lots of different things and test them to see whether they float or sink. You could test them in a large bowl of water, a sink or a bath. Make a chart showing which objects float and which sink. When you have tested everything look at the chart. Do the things which float have anything in common?

Things to test

needle
scissors
metal tray
empty tin can with a lid on
can of beans
plastic yogurt pot
dry bath sponge
wet bath sponge
cork
marble
ball of plasticine
ping-pong ball
wooden spoon
metal spoon
piece of wood

Water pushes back

Try to push a floater, such as a ping-pong ball, under water and it always bobs back. You can actually feel the water the ball pushes away, pushing back.

Why things float

Do things filled with air float or sink?

Try floating an empty bottle with its top on. Remember – the bottle looks empty but it is really full of air. Now take its top off and watch what happens.

Water pours into the bottle and pushes the air bubbles out of it. When all of the air has come out of the bottle, it sinks. The air was keeping it afloat before.

The more water something pushes away, the harder the water pushes up against it. A thing floats if the water pushes back strongly enough to support

18

You need a wide-necked jar and two balls of plasticine, a big one and a small one. Pour some water into the jar and mark the water level on it with a felt pen.

Drop the small ball of plasticine into the water and mark where the new water level comes to. Take the ball out and do the same thing with the bigger ball.

You will now have three marks showing the different water levels. The water level rises when you drop a ball into it because the ball pushes away the water to make room for itself. The bigger the ball is, the more water it has to push away and the higher the water level is.

You can feel how water tries to push things up if you stand chest deep in a pool with your arms by your sides. Let your arms go and they will slowly rise.

If you lift a rock out of water, it seems heavier out of the water than it does in it. Things feel lighter in water because the water helps to support them.

You can have great fun trying to sink a floater, such as an airbed or an inflated tyre. How many people can sit together on an airbed before it sinks?

You can make a sinker like a ball of plasticine float by making it into a bowl shape. If the bowl does not float at first, try making its sides higher.

The plasticine floats now because you have made it bigger on the outside than it was before. It pushes away more water, so the water pushes back harder.

A heavy ship has to push away a lot of water to float. The bigger the ship is, the more water it pushes away and the harder the water pushes back.

19

Shadowplay

Why do things have shadows? Play these games on a sunny day to find out all about shadows.

Does your shadow point towards the sun or away from it?

Play catch with your shadows.

Make a monster shadow . . .

Can you jump on your shadow?

Can you escape from your shadow?

Why has the shadow disappeared?

Why things have shadows

Light rays are straight. When rays of light are blocked by an object, a shadow appears. Ask a friend to shine a torch at a wall, then try making different shadows with your hands.

Shadow puzzle

What is wrong with this picture? Look carefully at all the shadows.

The shadows of the boats' masts, the runner, the tree, the dog and the car are facing the wrong way. The boy's shadow is in the wrong place. The shadows of the ball, building and boat are missing.

Shadow theatre

Entertain your friends with a shadow puppet theatre one evening when it is dark.

Make puppets by cutting scary figures out of thin card and taping them on to thin sticks.

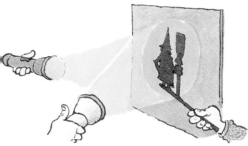

Hang a sheet across a doorway as a screen. The audience sits at one side of it and you and two friends on the other. One person holds the puppets while the others shine bright torches on them, to cast shadows on the screen. Move the torches backwards and forwards and watch what happens.

The nearer the torch is to an object, the more light you block and the bigger the shadow is.

If the torch is further away from the object more light can pass round it, so the shadow is smaller.

Making a shadow clock

Stand in a playground on a sunny morning and ask a friend to draw round your shoes and your shadow with chalk. Write down the time above your shadow.

Every two hours after that, stand with your feet in the same place and have your shadow drawn again. Write down the time above the shadow each time.

At the end of the day you will see that the position and shape of your shadow have changed. This is because the position of the sun changes during the day.

Reflections

Where do you see reflections? Collect shiny things – tiles, cans and bottles – and look at your reflection in them. When do you see the best reflections in water and windows? Look at your reflection in curved surfaces. What kinds of curves make things look thinner or fatter?

Mirror images

Look in a mirror and pull your right ear. Which ear does the image pull? A mirror reverses images from left to right.

Mirror code

Write a secret message to a friend in mirror code. No one else will be able to read it because it will be back to front.

Print the message on a piece of paper. Hold a mirror to one side of it and copy the reflected words on to another piece of paper.

Bouncing light

Try this experiment. You need two cardboard tubes, a torch and a mirror.

Reflections are caused by light bouncing off things. Try directing a beam of sunlight along a wall by reflecting it off a mirror.

Hold the mirror up near the edge of a table. Ask a friend to hold one tube at an angle to the mirror and to shine a torch down it.

Hold your tube next to the first one. Look through it and move it around until you see the light of the torch shining straight at you.

Look at your face in the bowl of a soup spoon. Hold the spoon at arm's length, then close up. What happens to your reflection?

Send this message to your friend. To decode it, all he has to do is hold a mirror to one side of it, as in the picture.

What happens

Look at where the tubes are, to see how the light moves. It shines down one tube and reflects off the mirror and up the other tube.

Multiple images

Tape two mirrors together, stand them up and put a toy between them. How many images can you see? What happens if you move the mirrors closer together?

If you have two big mirrors, stand them facing each other, then stand between them. Look in both mirrors and you will see endless reflections of yourself.

A kaleidoscope

The patterns in a kaleidoscope are made by mirrors reflecting off each other. To make a simple kaleidoscope you need three mirrors the same size, a piece of white card and bits of coloured paper.

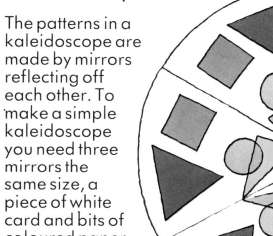

Tape the mirrors together, stand them on the card and draw round them. Cut out the triangle of card and tape it to the mirrors.

Drop the bits of paper into the kaleidoscope. How many pattern repeats can you see? Shake it to change the pattern.

Coloured light

Making rainbows

Fill a shallow dish with water. Put it by a window in the sun and slant a small mirror in it facing the sun. Hold a piece of paper above it and move the mirror until the sun shining through the water on to it is reflected on to the paper. You will see a rainbow.

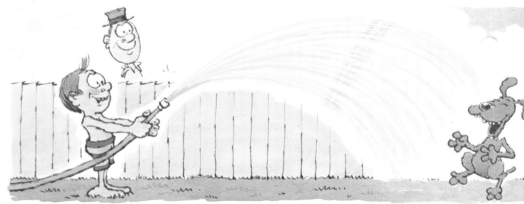

The colours you see in a rainbow are always in the same order. How many colours can you see and what are they? Where else do you see rainbow colours?

Light looks white but is really made of rainbow colours. The mirror and water split the light into colours and the mirror reflects them on to the paper.

Raindrops split sunlight. If you stand with your back to the sun, facing raindrops, you see a rainbow. Try making a rainbow with spray from a hose.

Disappearing colours

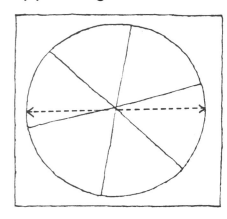

Draw a circle about 12 cm across on a piece of white card and draw lines across it to divide it into six equal parts.

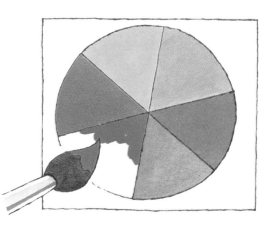

Paint each part a colour of the rainbow in the following order: red, orange, yellow, green, blue and violet. Let the paint dry.

Cut the circle out neatly and punch a hole in its centre with the tip of the scissors. Push a sharp pencil through the hole.

Changing the colour of the world

Make coloured viewers to look through. You need card for the frames, cellophane in different colours and sticky tape. You can make window viewers or spectacles. Look through the viewers. What happens to the colours you look at? Which colours change the most? What happens if you overlap different coloured viewers?

The viewers are a type of colour filter. They only let through light the same colour as themselves, so they stop you from seeing some of the other colours.

Stained glass windows act like colour filters. They filter the light shining through them, as you can see from the patterns they cast on the floor.

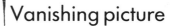

Vanishing picture

This trick works well if you have a red pen and a viewer exactly the same colour. Draw a picture with the pen on white paper, then look at it through the viewer. Where has the picture gone?

Answer: The filter makes you see the paper in the same colour as the picture.

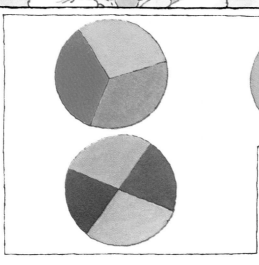

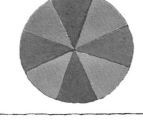

When a colour wheel spins fast, your eyes see the colours but your brain cannot separate them and you see a different colour.

Spin the wheel fast and watch what happens. Which colour or colours do you see? Make different coloured wheels and spin them. Make a chart showing the colour wheels and write under each one which colour you see when you spin it.

Spin a red and green wheel. Which colour do you see? Do you get the same colour if you mix green and red paint together?

Why do things make sounds?

MAKE YOUR OWN MUSICAL TOYS AND INSTRUMENTS AND EXPERIMENT WITH THE SOUNDS THEY MAKE

WHAT A CAT!

Stretch a long, thick rubber band round an empty coffee jar and pluck the bit across the top of the jar. Why does it make a sound?

Look at the rubber band and you will see it shaking. Try the same thing with another rubber band. Does it also make a sound?

Plucking and pinging

Stretch rubber bands round different things and pluck them. Do you always hear a sound? Do the rubber bands always shake?

What happens to the sound if you put your finger on a rubber band after you pluck it? Pluck the bands gently, then hard, to make soft and loud sounds. Do thick rubber bands make the same sound as thin ones?

Vibrations

When you pluck a rubber band, it shakes and makes the air around it shake. The air carries this shaking to your ear. Your eardrum shakes and you hear a sound.

This shaking is called vibration. Try these experiments to see how other things also make sounds by vibrating.

Sprinkle grains of rice on a drum. Beat the drum and the rice dances around because the drumskin shakes.

How sound travels

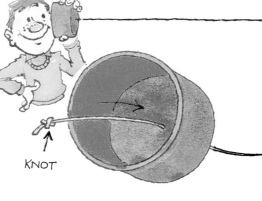

KNOT

Make this telephone and talk to your friends through it. You need two yogurt pots and a long piece of thin string.

Punch a small hole in the base of each yogurt pot. Push one end of the string through the base of one pot and tie a big knot in it. Then do the same with the other pot.

High sounds and low sounds

YOU CAN PLAY TUNES ON THIS RUBBER BAND HARP

You need a plastic box and eight thick rubber bands. Stretch the rubber bands round the box, then tighten them, by catching them on the edge of the box, to give each one a different note. The tighter the rubber band, the higher the note it makes. Try tuning the rubber bands so you can play a scale.

Find some bottles the same size. Pour different amounts of water into them and tap them. How can you give a bottle a higher note?

Watch how musicians tune their guitars and violins by tightening the strings.

Hang a saucepan lid from a piece of string. Tap it with a spoon, listen and watch.

HHUUUMMMM!

Put your hand on your throat and hum a tune. What do you feel?

Hold a ruler down on the edge of a table and twang it. Does the sound change if you make the twanging end shorter?

For the telephone to work, the string must be pulled tight and not touch anything. Whisper into your yogurt pot while your friend holds his close to his ear.

Your friend can hear what you say because your voice makes the string vibrate and the vibration travels along it to the other yogurt pot. The sound of your voice travels better through the string than it does through air.

What is gravity?

Things do not move by themselves. They stay where they are unless something pushes or pulls them. When you kick a ball you make it go up in the air. But what makes it come back down to the ground?

The Earth pulls things towards it. This pull is called gravity. It makes the ball fall back to the ground, leaves fall from the tree and streams run downhill.

Weighing things

Make this spring scale and you can compare how much things weigh. Try to guess which things are heaviest before you weigh them.

You need
a yogurt pot
a thin rubber band
2 bits of wire both the same length
2 paper clips
a strip of white card

Punch two holes in the top of the yogurt pot and hook the bits of wire through them. Twist them together to make a handle with a hook at the top.

Hook the paper clips together and clip the bottom one to the card. Hang the rubber band from it and hook the yogurt pot on to it.

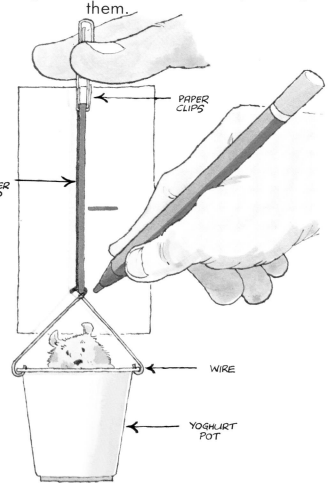

PAPER CLIPS

RUBBER BAND

WIRE

YOGHURT POT

Spring scales are often used to weigh wild animals. They are put to sleep first.

Put things in the yogurt pot to weigh them. Mark how far down the card the wire hook comes so that you can compare weights.

Things have weight because of the pull of gravity on them. The greater the pull of gravity on an object, the more it weighs.

A see-saw works like scales. How could the children help make the see-saw balance?

28

Gravity and movement

People often make use of gravity to make things move downhill.

Balancing tricks

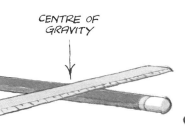

CENTRE OF GRAVITY

You can make a ruler balance on a pencil. At one point it acts as if all its weight were on the pencil because its two ends weigh the same and balance each other.

The balancing point of an object is called its centre of gravity. Try these balancing tricks.

Balancing Potato

Push two identical forks into either side of a raw potato, as shown. Move them around a bit and you can make the potato balance on the edge of a glass.

Balancing a needle

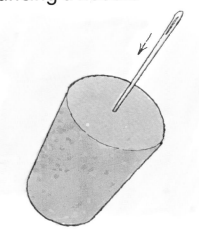

To do this you need a needle, a cork, a lump of plasticine and 20-30 cm of thin, stiff wire. Push the needle into the cork.

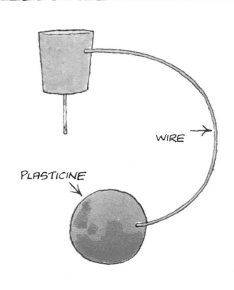

WIRE

PLASTICINE

Bend the wire into a curve. Push one end of it into the side of the cork and the other end into the ball of plasticine.

Stand the needle on the edge of a shelf. It balances as if by magic!

Bounces and springs

What makes a ball bounce? Where does its energy or 'go' come from? Bounce a rubber ball. How high can you make it bounce? How long does it carry on bouncing? Count the bounces and watch how high they are. Make a paper marker to help you measure how high the ball bounces. Drop the ball from different heights and ask a friend to mark how high it bounces.

Testing for bounce

Test different balls to see which one bounces best. Drop them all from the same height and measure the height of the first bounce. Make a chart showing how high each ball bounces. Which is the best bouncer? Look at its size and shape. What is it made of?

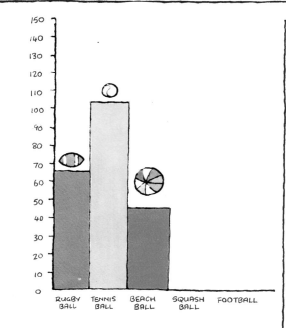

The plasticine test

Does a rubber ball's shape change when you bounce it on a hard floor? What happens when you drop a ball of plasticine on the floor?

All the plasticine's 'go' is used up when it splats on the ground. If you drop a rubber ball on soft sand its energy is used up making a dent in the sand. A ball bounces best when both it and the surface on which it falls keep their shape.

Test your best bouncer on different surfaces – a hard floor, a carpet, grass and sand – to see where it bounces best. Always drop it from the same height to keep the test fair. Does the ball ever mark the surface? Does it still bounce well if this happens?

Energy from rubber and springs

If you stretch a piece of elastic and let go of one end, it springs back into place. You can use this energy to catapult things.

Springs can also make things move because they stretch, then spring back into place. Pop-up toys often have a spring.

A slinky *is* a spring. Make one move down some steps and watch how it stretches, then squeezes back together again.

Creeping toy

You need
an empty cotton reel
a candle
a rubber band
a matchstick
a thin stick about 10 cm long
scissors and a knife
sticky tape

1.

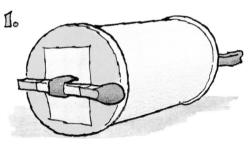

Push the rubber band through the cotton reel. Push a bit of matchstick through the loop at one end and tape it down.

2.

Slice a ring off the end of the candle and make a small hole in the middle with the scissors.

WIND UP

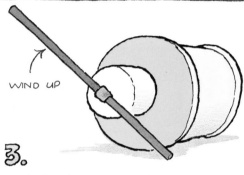

3.

Push the free end of the rubber band through the bit of candle. Push the stick through the loop.

Wind the stick round and put the toy down. It looks really creepy if you put a handkerchief over it.

How the toy works

The toy moves as its rubber band 'motor' unwinds. If you have a clockwork toy wind it up and watch what happens to its spring when the toy works.

Simple machines

For thousands of years people have made work easier by using machines to help them move heavy things. Make these simple machines and see how they work.

A lever helps you to lift heavy things easily. Make one by laying a short plank over a tin. Balance the plank so the lever has a short end and a long end.

Now try lifting some bricks with it. Put them first on the long end, then on the short end of the lever. When do you find it easiest to lift them?

A lever works like a see-saw. You can lift a heavy weight on the short end by pushing down on the long end. You do not have to push down with the same weight as the load, but you have to push further.

If you have a strong plank and a thick, round stick you can lift a friend on a chair. Set up the lever as in the picture. Try lifting your friend by pressing down on the plank near to the chair, then further away. When is it easiest to lift the chair?

Levers round the house

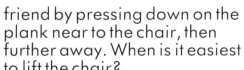

Push the lid of a tin firmly into place, then try opening it with a coin. Now try again with a screwdriver. Which opens the lid more easily?

A door acts like a lever. It moves round the hinge. Try closing one by pushing it near the hinge, then near the handle. When do you have to push hardest?

A wheelbarrow is another type of lever and helps you to lift things you would not normally be strong enough to lift. The wheel acts as the balancing point.

Pulleys

When you use a simple pulley, you pull downwards to lift an object up, using your weight to help you. With a pulley like the one above you can lift an object which weighs as much as you.

Pulley puzzle

Mighty Max weighs 100 kilos. Which weights can he lift using a pulley like the one above?

What makes a crane so strong? Look at the number of pulleys the wire cable goes round.

Who is strongest?

Do this trick with four friends. You need two brooms and a long rope. Tie one end of the rope to a broom, then loop it from one broom to the other, as in the picture.

Ask your friends to try and pull the brooms apart, while you pull on the free end of the rope. Who is the stronger?

The brooms act like pulleys. The more times the rope goes round the brooms, the stronger your pulling power. The trick works even better if you dust the broom handles with talcum powder, so that the rope can slide easily.

Gears and pulleys

The chain wheel and rear sprocket of your bicycle act like pulleys connected by a belt (the chain). Why do you think they are different sizes? Study your bike.

How many turns does the back wheel make for every turn of the chain wheel? How many turns does the chain wheel make for one turn of the wheel?

Magnetic powers

Magnets attract things as if by magic. Do these experiments to find out about their strange powers. Use horseshoe magnets or, even better, bar magnets.

Which things are attracted to a magnet? Go round a room testing a magnet against different things.

Collect small objects, such as pins and paper clips and make a list of the things your magnet will pick up. Are they all made of metal?

Test the pulling power of your magnet. Can you pick an object up by holding the magnet just above it? What do you feel when you pull something off a magnet

ARE MAGNETS ATTRACTED TO WOOD?

Does a magnet work through glass? Drop a paper clip in a glass of water. Hold a magnet against the glass and try sliding the paper clip up to the top.

Treasure Hunt

Put some small metal objects, such as screws and nuts, on a plastic tray and cover them with dry sand or sawdust. Use a magnet to detect where they are.

Magnet maze game

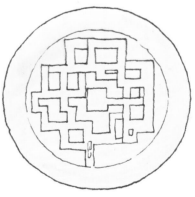

To play this game you need a bar magnet, a paper plate and a paper clip. Draw a maze or wiggly path on the plate. One person holds up the plate. The

others take it in turn to hold the magnet under the plate and to try and guide the paper clip through the maze or along the path without touching any lines.

The poles of a magnet

Dip a magnet into a pile of paper clips. Which part of the magnet do the clips cling to? The ends of a magnet are called the poles. Are they stronger than the middle?

See if you can pick up a chain of paper clips with one end of the magnet. How long a chain can you make? What happens to it if you take it off the magnet?

Making a magnet

Hold the needle in one hand. Stroke it gently 10 times in one direction with one end of the magnet. Now see if you can pick up some pins with the needle.

Pushing and pulling

Try this experiment to see what magnets do when you put them together. Put two toy railway trucks about 2 cm apart on some straight railway track. Put a bar magnet in each truck and watch what happens. Turn one magnet round and repeat the experiment.

Finding North

Float a bar magnet on a polystyrene tray in a bowl of water. The bowl should be big enough for the tray to float freely, so that it can find its own direction.

Hold the magnets close together and you can feel what happens. The two ends of a magnet are different. One end of one magnet attracts or pulls one end of the second magnet towards it, but its other end pushes it away.

The tray will turn until one end of the magnet points to the North. A single magnet which can float freely, and which is not near iron, acts as a compass needle.

Crackles and sparks

There are two sorts of electricity: one that stays in the same place and one that flows through thing
You can make the first sort, static electricity, by rubbing things together. Do these experiments
and strange things will happen.

Magic Comb Tricks

Charge a clean plastic comb with electricity by combing your hair hard when it is clean. Hold the comb above your head.

Turn on a tap until there is a steady trickle of water. Hold the charged comb near the water and watch what happens.

Making sparks

By rubbing the tray on the bag, you make electricity and when there is enough electricity it makes a spark. Static electricity builds up in clouds before a storm. Flashes of lightning are giant sparks of electricity.

Press a lump of plasticine firmly on to a tin baking tray. Hold the plasticine lump and rub the tray round and round on a big, thick plastic or polythene bag.

Lift the tray up and hold a metal object, such as a tin lid, close to one corner. You will see a spark jump from the tray to the tin, especially if the room is dark.

Mrs Brown cannot carry on with her housework because there is a power cut. How many things in the picture have stopped working? (Look for things that run on electricity).

It lights!

The electricity that is used to run machinery is called current electricity because it can flow through things. Find out how it works by making this simple circuit.

You need
a 4.5v torch battery
a 3.5v bulb and a bulb holder
3 pieces of single strand flex
a small screwdriver

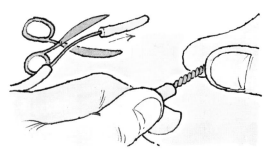

Cut about 2 cm of plastic from the ends of each piece of flex and twist the little wires together to make neat ends.

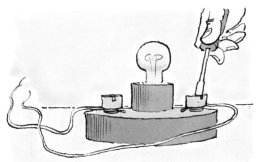

Undo the screws of the bulb holder slightly. Hook the ends of two pieces of flex round them. Tighten the screws. Screw in the bulb.

Hook the other ends of the flexes to the battery terminals and the bulb will light. Electricity runs from the battery along a flex to the bulb, then up the other flex to

the battery. Its path is called a circuit. If you unhook a flex from one of the battery terminals, the light goes out because you have broken the circuit.

Does electricity only flow through wires?

Test different things to see if electricity will flow through any of them. Test lots of things and write down your results.

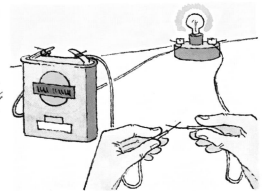

Use three pieces of flex for this test. Join them as in the picture. If you hold the two loose ends of flex together, the bulb lights, showing you have a circuit.

Hold the ends of each object you want to test against the two loose wires, as shown. If electricity can flow through the object, the bulb lights again.

Glossary

attract Pull towards (p. 34).

centre of gravity The point at which an object balances perfectly (p. 29).

condensation Tiny drops of water you see on cold things. They form when water vapour in the air cools and turns back into water, or condenses (p. 12).

electricity A form of energy that is easy to use. There are two sorts of electricity: static electricity, which stays in one place, and current electricity, which can flow through things (pp. 36/37).

energy The 'go' in things, whatever makes them work (p. 30).

evaporate Dry up and change into vapour that you cannot see (p. 10).

expand Grow bigger (p. 8).

filter A screen which only allows certain colours to pass through it (p. 25).

fluid Runny, like water (p. 14).

gravity The pull of the Earth (p. 28).

image Reflection (p. 22).

kaleidoscope A toy in which reflections from mirrors make patterns (p. 23).

lever A straight bar which makes it easier to lift heavy things (p. 32).

liquid A runny substance, such as water, which spreads out to fill whatever container it is in (p. 14).

machine Any object that helps to make work easier (p. 32).

magnet An object which can attract certain metals (p. 34).

multiple Many.

poles The ends of a magnet, where the power seems strongest (p. 35).

pulley A grooved wheel over which a rope passes. It is used to lift heavy things (p. 33).

reflection The light or image you see when light bounces off a surface (p. 22).

siphon A bent tube used to move liquid from one place to another (p. 15).

transparent See-through.

vibrate Move quickly backwards and forwards (p. 26).

water vapour The gas that water turns into when it dries up. It is made of droplets of water which are so small that you cannot see them (p. 10).

Simple Science Quiz

Here is a quiz about this section of the book. See how much you can remember. You could either write down your answers and then check them against those on page 40, or you could have a quiz with somebody else. Some of the questions ask you to choose the correct word to describe something. Always make sure that you read the words carefully, as some have been added to try to catch you out. If you find that you don't understand the question, or that you get the answer wrong, just turn to the page mentioned in the answer. Reading the suggested page again should help you to understand.

1 Which will fall to the ground faster; a playing card dropped face-down or a playing card dropped end on?

2 If a hot air balloon pilot wants to land, does he heat up the air in the balloon, or does he leave the air to cool?

3 If you leave a hot drink in a room for a long time, would the temperature of the drink become hotter, colder or the same as the air temperature of the room?

4 Why do farmers shear their sheep in the summer and not in the winter?

5 When a puddle dries up, has the water evaporated or melted?

6 Is water vapour another name for rain, or the gas that water turns into when it dries up?

7 What is the best weather for drying clothes; sunny and windy, or cloudy and windy?

8 Is steam made up of droplets of smoke, or droplets of water?

9 What do you call the mist that appears on mirrors at bathtime; fog or condensation?

10 What do you call the water vapour in clouds when it is frozen into crystals?

11 What is wrong with this sentence? The river flowed up the hill to the sea.

12 If you make water flow from one jar to another, through a tube, have you made a lever, a siphon or a filter?

13 Why are the insects called pond-skaters able to walk over the surface of a pond?

14 Which of these things will not float; a ping-pong ball, a rubber ring or a pair of scissors?

15 Which will float; a piece of plasticine shaped like a bowl, or a piece of plasticine shaped like a ball?

16 Why can't you see your shadow on a cloudy day?

17 When is your shadow longer; at breakfast time or at midday?

18 What do you need to use in order to read this message?

I like science.

19 When you look in the mirror, do you see a reflection, a reflector or a monster?

20 What is the name for a device made by taping three mirrors together to show repeated patterns? Is it a periscope, a telescope or a kaleidoscope?

21 If you want to see a rainbow, do you have to stand with your back to the sun facing the raindrops, or with your back to the raindrops facing the sun?

22 Which part of your ear shakes when you hear sounds?

23 When you throw something up into the air, it always falls back down to earth. What is the name of the force that makes this happen?

24 Are spring scales used to measure weight, or the temperature on a spring day?

25 Where would a ball bounce highest; on an airport runway or on a sandy beach?

26 Which of these things do not use a pulley; a wall, a crane or a wheelbarrow?

27 Will a magnet work through a paper plate?

28 Are flashes of lightning made by light bouncing off raindrops, or by giant sparks of electricity?

29 Can you think of five things in your home that work by using electricity?

Simple Science Answers

1   A playing card dropped end on will fall to the ground faster than a playing card dropped face-down. This is because the air pushes up under the flat card and slows it down. See page 7.

2   The pilot would leave the air to cool. (Hot air would make the balloon rise.) See page 8.

3   If you leave a hot drink in a room for a long time, it would reach the same temperature as the air in the room. See page 9.

4   Farmers do not shear sheep in winter because wool traps air and keeps sheep warm in cold weather. See page 9.

5   The water from a dried-up puddle has evaporated. See page 10.

6   Water vapour is another name for the gas that water turns into when it dries up. See page 10.

7   A sunny, windy day is the best weather for drying clothes because the sun helps the water to evaporate more quickly. See page 11.

8   Steam is made up of droplets of water. (Smoke is made when something is burned.) See page 12.

9   The mist on mirrors at bathtime is called condensation. (Fog is cloud that is very near the ground.) See page 13.

10   In clouds, the water vapour that has frozen into crystals is called snow. See page 13.

11   Water cannot flow upwards. The sentence should read, "The river flowed DOWN the hill to the sea." See page 14.

12   This type of device is called a siphon. (A lever is something that you use to lift heavy things, and a filter is a screen which only allows certain things to pass through.) See page 15.

13   The pond's surface is covered with a type of skin, called surface tension. This is strong enough to support the pond-skaters as they skim across the water. See page 16.

14   A pair of scissors will not float, but a ping-pong ball and a rubber ring will. See page 19.

15   A piece of plasticine shaped like a bowl will float, but a piece of plasticine shaped like a ball will not because the bowl shape pushes away more water than the ball. See page 19.

16   You can't see your shadow on a cloudy day because your shadow is made by your body blocking out the light of the sun. See page 20.

17   Your shadow is longer at breakfast time. The shortest shadows are made when the sun is overhead. This usually happens at around midday. See page 21.

18   You need to use a mirror to read this message. See page 22.

19   You see your reflection in a mirror. (I hope you are not a monster. A reflector is a red or orange plastic circle on the back of a bike. It lights up when you shine a light on it.) See page 22.

20   This type of device, with at least three mirrors, is called a kaleidoscope. (A periscope is used on a submarine to see things above the water and a telescope is used to see objects in the distance.) See page 23.

21   You have to stand with your back to the sun, facing the raindrops, if you want to see a rainbow. See page 24.

22   It is your eardrum that shakes when you hear sounds. See page 26.

23   The force that makes things fall back to earth is called gravity. See page 28.

24   Spring scales are used to measure weight. See page 28.

25   A ball bounces better on a hard surface than on sand, so it would bounce higher on the airport runway than on the beach. See page 30.

26   A well and a crane both use a pulley; a wheelbarrow does not. Wheelbarrows use a lever. See page 33.

27   Yes, a magnet will work through a paper plate. See page 34.

28   Flashes of lightning are giant sparks of electricity. (Light bouncing off raindrops can make a rainbow.) See page 36.

29   Anything that has a plug on it or that uses batteries is powered by electricity. See page 36.

LIVING THINGS

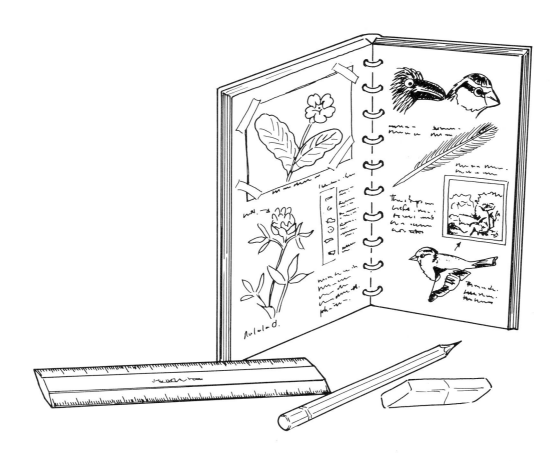

LIVING THINGS

Marit Claridge

Illustrated by John Shackell

Designed by Anne Sharples

Consultant: Gillian Ghate

Contents

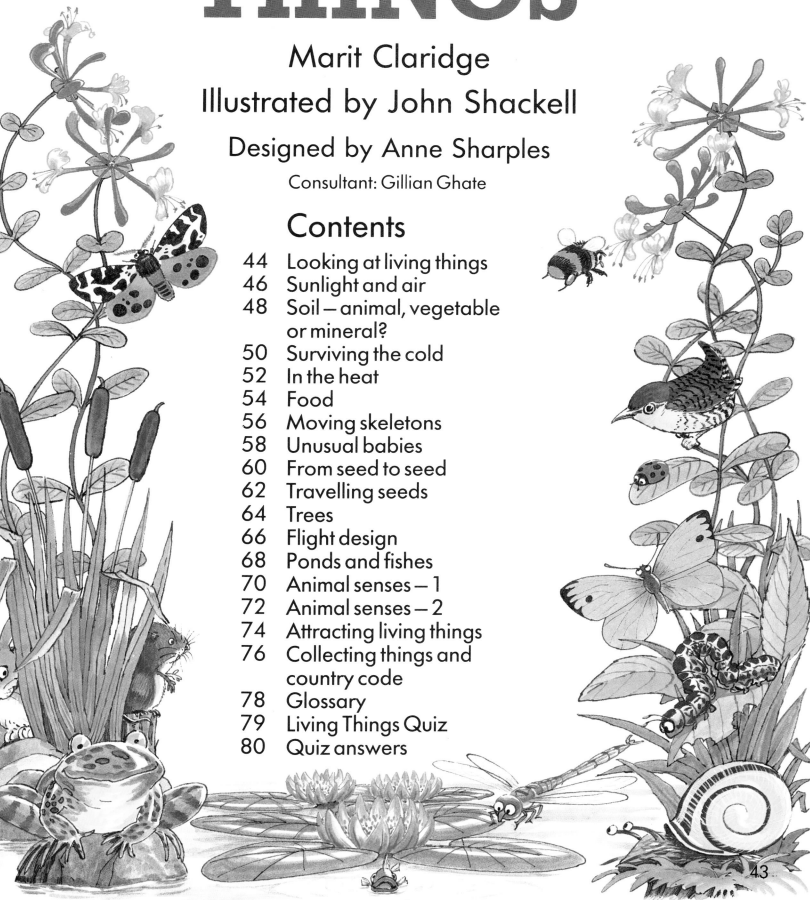

Looking at living things

Living things are all around you – in the sky, in the garden, in your home, in water. Have you ever wondered how they live and what they do?

HOW DO BIRDS FLY?

WHY DO TREES LOSE THEIR LEAVES?

WHAT ARE BONES FOR?

DO PLANTS MOVE?

WHAT ARE FEATHERS FOR?

WHY DO SHEEP EAT ALL DAY?

ARE WORMS USEFUL?

WHY IS THIS GRASS YELLOW?

WHY DO PLANTS HAVE FLOWERS?

DOES FOOD GIVE YOU ENERGY?

WHAT DO PLANTS EAT?

WHY DO APPLES HAVE PIPS?

ARE TWO EYES BETTER THAN ONE?

HOW DO CATERPILLARS TURN INTO BUTTERFLIES?

DO CATS FEEL WITH THEIR WHISKERS?

WHAT LIVES IN THIS POND?

HOW DO FISHES BREATHE?

44

What is biology?

Biology is the study of nature and all living things. Biologists are interested in how the bodies of plants, animals and human beings work, and the way they live.

Biologists ask questions about plants and animals and then try to work out the answers. You can do this too. There are lots of simple tests and experiments you can try to find out more about living things around you.

Some biology experiments can take a long time, so you need to be very patient. If an experiment does not work the first time, try doing it again.

Start a biology scrapbook

Write up your experiments in a scrapbook. Draw what happens at each stage, and note how long it takes.

You will find most of the things you need for the experiments in your home.

Using your eyes

You can learn a lot about living things by watching carefully. Look for living things wherever you go — they may be difficult to spot.

You don't need to buy expensive equipment, but a magnifying glass is very useful for looking close-up at things.

Try to sketch the things you see where they live rather than killing them by bringing them home.

Sunlight and air

Do plants need sunlight?

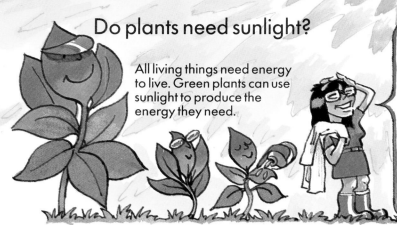

All living things need energy to live. Green plants can use sunlight to produce the energy they need.

Leaves are green because they contain green colouring matter called chlorophyll. Chlorophyll soaks up energy from the sunlight.

A gas in the air, called carbon dioxide, enters leaves through tiny holes. It mixes with water which has been drawn up by the roots. Sunlight changes the mixture of carbon dioxide and water into sugar and starch, and oxygen, another gas, is given off into the air. This process is called photosynthesis.

Oxygen makers

If you put a jar of pondweed in the sun, you will see lots of bubbles rise in the water. These are bubbles of oxygen.

POND-WEED

Buy pondweed in a pet shop.

Do plants breathe?

Try this test to find out whether plants breathe.

Soak two beans for 3 to 4 days.

Put some wet cotton wool or kitchen towel in a jar and place the beans on top.

Water the jar each day and when the beans have grown roots and shoots, screw the lid tightly on the jar. Put the jar in a dark place for two days.

Light a long, thin, dry stick and put it into the jar.

The flame goes out. Things need oxygen to burn and this test shows that there is very little oxygen in the jar or the flame would stay alight.

The beans use up the oxygen in the jar and give off carbon dioxide, which shows that they do breathe.

Balancing the air

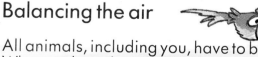

All animals, including you, have to breathe to live. When we breathe in, our bodies use the oxygen in the air and make carbon dioxide which we breathe out. During the day, plants help to replace the oxygen by photosynthesis.

Fires also use up oxygen.

Some scientists believe that if all the world's forests were cut down, all the oxygen in the air would eventually be used up.

Does sunlight make leaves green?

Sprinkle some cress seeds into two dishes lined with damp kitchen paper. Put one dish in a light place and the other in a dark cupboard.

Keep the soil damp using a fine spray.

After 3 or 4 days the seedlings growing in the light will be green and healthy, but those in the dark will be yellow.

The seedlings which grew in the dark cupboard will also be taller because they grow upwards to find light.

The chlorophyll in leaves is made by a reaction with the sunlight. Without the chlorophyll the leaves would be yellow.

Sunworshippers

Plants grow to catch as much sunlight as possible. Watch what happens to pot plants on a sunny window-sill.

The leaves turn to face the light.

The heads of sunflowers turn to face the sun and follow its path through the day.

The flower itself cannot photosynthesize, but when the leaves turn to face the sun, the head turns too.

What happens if you turn the plant round?

Which part of the plant is sensitive to light?

Try this test to find out. Sow some oat seeds in two separate dishes and wait for them to grow.

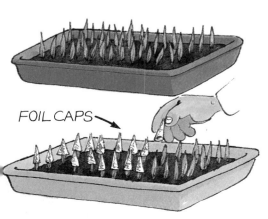

FOIL CAPS

When they are about 3cm high, cover the tips of the seedlings in one of the dishes with tiny silver foil caps. Place both of the dishes near a window and wait to see what happens.

The capped seedlings will grow up straight and the seedlings without caps bend towards the light. This shows that it is the tips of the seedlings that are sensitive to light.

WITHOUT CAPS

WITH CAPS

Soil — animal, vegetable or mineral?

Soil may just look like mud but it is made up of many different things. Dig up some soil from under a bush to see what it is made of. Put it in a jar with water, stir it and leave it to settle for a day.

It will fall into separate layers.

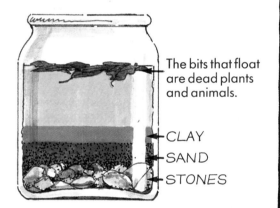

The bits that float are dead plants and animals.

- CLAY
- SAND
- STONES

The stones, sand and clay come from rock which has been worn down by wind and water over millions of years. This is called weathering.

Rot and decay

Dead plants and animals rot and become part of the soil. Rotting is caused by bacteria and fungi which grow on the dead bodies. They break the bodies down into minerals. Other minerals in soil come from weathered rocks.

Worm gardeners

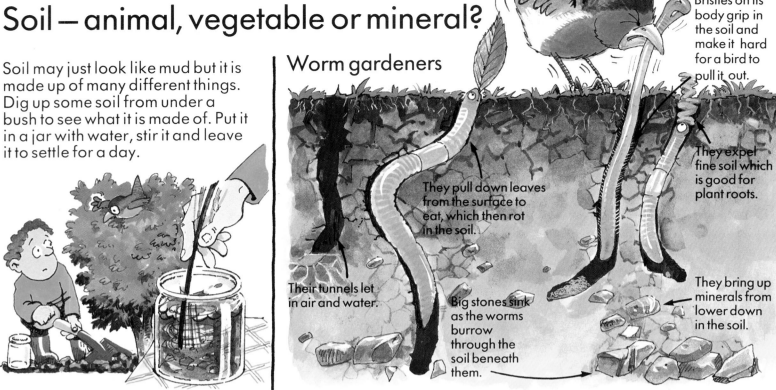

Bristles on its body grip in the soil and make it hard for a bird to pull it out.

They pull down leaves from the surface to eat, which then rot in the soil.

They expel fine soil which is good for plant roots.

Their tunnels let in air and water.

Big stones sink as the worms burrow through the soil beneath them.

They bring up minerals from lower down in the soil.

Worms eat the rotting plants in the soil. As they eat their way through soil, they improve it for plants in several ways.

A wormery jar

Gently dig over a patch of soil — you will soon come across some worms.

Fill a jar with layers of damp sand and soil and put leaves on top. Add two worms. Cover the jar with dark cloth.

Look after a few days. You will see how the worms have mixed up the layers.

Worm charming

Worms come to the surface to breathe when it rains heavily, they might otherwise drown in water-logged soil.

If you bang on a lawn, worms may come up, thinking that it is raining.

WORM

ANT

EARWIG

MILLIPEDE

WOODLOUSE

SLUG

All kinds of different animals live in soil and rotting leaves, from minute ones which eat bacteria, to bigger ones such as earthworms and beetles.

CENTIPEDE

Look in rotting leaves for some of these animals.

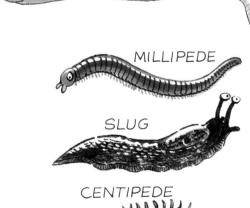

Do plants need soil?

Plants, like animals, cannot grow without food and water.

Green plants make the food they need through their leaves by using sunlight, but they also need soil for its minerals and nutrients. Soil also protects seeds from cold in the winter.

Plants need soil as an "anchor" for their roots.

Dig up a weed and look closely at its roots. They are covered in lots of tiny hairs.

Plants "drink" up minerals and water through these tiny hairs.

Feeding soil

Where plants, such as trees in jungles, grow undisturbed, their fallen leaves, fruits, and branches give the soil back minerals which have been taken up in the plant's roots.

The plants feed the soil, and the soil in turn feeds the plants.

Why do farmers need fertilizers?

Farmers use the same soil over and over again to grow crops which are then cut down and taken away. The soil becomes poorer and lacks the minerals that plants need.

Farmers add fertilizers to the soil which put back many of the lost minerals.

Animal manure is good for the soil too. Can you think why?

In the garden

Gardeners sometimes dig decayed plants, called compost, into the soil to replace the goodness plants have taken out.

The inside of the heap gets warm as the bacteria rots down the plants.

Compost heaps can be made in a corner of the garden with fruit skins, old vegetables, grass cuttings and other cut plants.

Surviving the cold

As summer weather cools in autumn, plants and animals in many parts of the world prepare for cold winter weather.

Mammals, including human beings and birds, are "warm-blooded". The food they eat acts like fuel to keep their bodies warm.

Some birds cannot find enough food during cold weather in the same place as they breed in summer.

You may see birds, such as swallows or martins, gathering on telephone wires at the end of summer. They fly south together to warmer places where they can find food. They return in the spring.

FLUFFED UP FEATHERS

In cold weather birds use their feathers to keep warm. Feathers trap a layer of air close to their bodies. They can fluff them up and tuck in their naked legs and beaks to keep warm.

Mammals have a coat of fur, wool or hair which helps to keep them warm. Furry animals can fluff up their fur in a similar way to a bird's feathers.

Air trapped in feathers and fur keeps birds and animals warm. Air is an insulator, which means it keeps in heat.

What are goose-pimples?

Muscles under the skin make fur and feathers stand on end. We have "goose-pimples" when we are cold which are made in the same way even though we have very little hair on our bodies.

You need clothes to keep your body warm. You will be warmer on a cold day with a few loose layers of clothes than one, thick layer. More layers trap more air.

About a quarter of your body heat is lost through your head.

Blue with cold

Heat is carried around your body by your blood. When you are cold, blood vessels near the surface of your skin contract. This moves warm blood away from your skin so you lose less heat to the air.

You look blue or white because you have less red blood near the surface of your skin.

Extra underwear

Seals have thin fur, but an extra thick fat layer keeps them warm in icy seas.

Animals that live in places that are always cold, such as penguins in the Antarctic, have a thick layer of fat, called blubber, beneath their skins to keep them warm.

Deep sleep

Some animals, such as the dormouse, cannot find enough food to eat in winter.

In the autumn it eats a lot while there is still plenty of food about. Its body builds up a layer of fat to feed off during the winter.

It finds a safe shelter and goes into a deep sleep until the weather warms up. This is called hibernation. When a mammal hibernates, its body temperature

HIBERNATING DORMOUSE

falls well below normal and its breathing becomes slow and irregular. Its body works slowly, using the stored food.

Do plants die in winter?

Many plants die at the end of summer.

Plants, such as poppies, cannot survive the cold weather. Their roots are not able to draw up water from frozen soil and their leaves and stems are damaged by frost.

The seeds fall through holes in the top of the pod and are blown away by the wind.

A poppy dies after it has produced seeds at the end of summer, but the plant survives in the form of seeds. The seeds which land on soil may grow into a new poppy in spring.

Why do some trees lose their leaves?

Trees lose water through their leaves. In summer this water is replaced by water drawn up through their roots.

Trees which lose their leaves in winter are called deciduous trees.

If the ground is cold or frozen, a tree's roots cannot draw up water. It sheds its leaves in autumn to stop it from losing all of its water.

BRANCH OF CONIFER

Some trees, called coniferous trees, keep most of their leaves in winter. They have small, tough, waxy leaves, which limits the amount of water they can lose.

Underground larder

Some plants, such as potatoes and daffodils, survive the winter underground with their own supply of food. The plants use the food store in spring for growing and flowering.

Daffodils store their food in bulbs. These contain buds which are ready to grow in spring.

Onions are also bulbs. Cut one in half and look for the small bud which is ready to sprout into a new plant.

When a potato plant dies down at the end of summer, it stores food in swollen stems – these are the potatoes. Each potato can produce a new plant in spring.

In the heat

In hot weather, plants lose a lot of water through their leaves. If this water is not replaced, they die.

Why is water necessary?

Plants need water to carry minerals up from the soil and for photosynthesis. Water also keeps the stems and leaves of non-woody plants rigid.

CELERY

COLOURED WATER

If you forget to water a plant it will droop. The plant will recover if you water it before it has died.

Water is drawn up through the plant's roots and travels up the stem to the leaves and flowers.

If you put a stick of celery in water coloured with food colouring, you can see that the water travels up the stem.

Prove that plants give off water

Cover a well-watered pot plant with a clear plastic bag. Tie it down around the pot so that air cannot get into the bag.

After a few hours, the inside of the bag will be coated with drops of water.

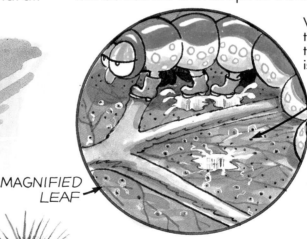

Water comes out through tiny holes, called stomata, in the leaves. This loss of water is called transpiration.

Put the plant in a sunny place.

MAGNIFIED LEAF

Extra protection

Plants grow well in jungles where it is hot and there is also a lot of rain.

In some parts of the world it is very hot but it hardly ever rains. Plants in these areas need to protect themselves from losing water.

A waxy skin helps to keep in the water.

Cacti store water in their thick stems. They can also store water in their roots. The roots spread over large areas or go down very deep to reach as much water as possible.

Cacti either have no leaves, or have tiny spines instead of leaves. They only have very few stomata on their stems.

The spines keep off thirsty animals.

On a hot day a tree can "drink" as much as 50 buckets of water through its roots. Most of this comes out invisibly through its leaves.

Keeping cool

Your body needs to stay at a temperature of about 37°C. If your body gets very hot, you could become ill.

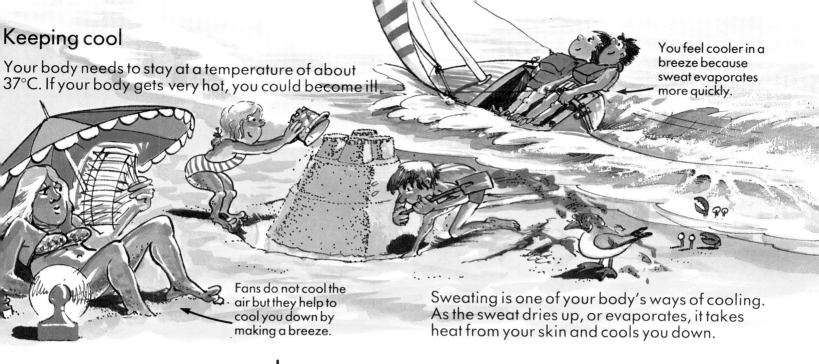

You feel cooler in a breeze because sweat evaporates more quickly.

Fans do not cool the air but they help to cool you down by making a breeze.

Sweating is one of your body's ways of cooling. As the sweat dries up, or evaporates, it takes heat from your skin and cools you down.

Getting in a sweat

If you look at your palm or the skin inside your elbow through a magnifying glass, you can see tiny holes in the skin, called pores.

Sweat comes out through the pores.

Have you noticed how you look red and your veins stick out when you are hot?

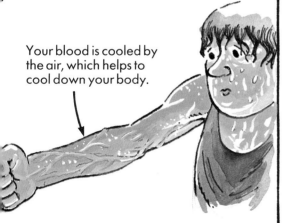

Your blood is cooled by the air, which helps to cool down your body.

Blood vessels near the surface of your skin widen when you are hot so that more blood flows near the surface.

A waterproof skin

When you get wet, water drips off you because your skin is waterproof.

A drink helps to replace the water lost through sweating.

You lose sweat through your pores but your waterproof skin stops you losing too much.

Nearly three-quarters of your body is water. Water is needed to keep you alive and healthy.

How do animals keep cool?

Some animals, such as elephants, have very large ears. These are full of tiny blood vessels which are cooled in the air.

Slowly flapping its ears in the air helps to keep the elephant cool and comfortable.

If you see a dog resting after a run, it will probably be panting.

A dog cannot sweat. Instead water evaporates from its tongue and cools it down.

Food

Food gives your body the things it needs to heal cuts and scratches.

Food gives you energy to play and run about.

All animals, including you, need food. Food helps you to grow, to keep healthy and to give you the energy to run about, play games and lots of other things.

Some animals, such as cows, sheep and rabbits, only eat plants. They are called herbivores. Other animals, such as lions, cats and dogs, only eat meat. They are called carnivores. People are able to eat both plants and meat and are called omnivores.

Herbivores and carnivores

When you see herbivores, they always seem to be eating. But if you have a cat or dog, you will know it only has one or two meals a day.

A SHEEP EATS FOR ABOUT 20 HOURS A DAY

Why do herbivores eat more than carnivores? Which is more filling – a plateful of meat or a plateful of lettuce?

Plants contain a special substance called cellulose which is very tough. You cannot live on grass because your body cannot use the cellulose.

MAGNIFIED PLANT STEM

Lions rest while their bodies digest large meals.

Cows, and other herbivores, have special bacteria living in their stomachs which break the cellulose down into food their bodies can use. This is called digestion.

They need to eat a huge amount of plant food to get enough nourishment from it.

Meat is easy to digest and full of nourishment, so lions and other carnivores may only eat once every three days.

Your teeth

When you eat a mouthful of food, the first thing you do is to bite and chew it.

You have two main types of teeth. The sharp ones in front are for biting. They are called incisors and canines.

Your back teeth are for crushing and grinding up the food. They are called premolars and molars.

If you look at a cat's or dog's teeth, you will see that their canines are very long and pointed. Carnivores need these to rip up raw meat. Their premolars and molars are also sharper than yours.

FLAT, RIDGED TEETH

SHARP, POINTED CANINES

Horses are herbivores. Their teeth are flat and ridged for chewing grass and hay.

What do you eat?

You need to eat a variety of different kinds of foods because they do different jobs in your body. Some foods do more than one job.

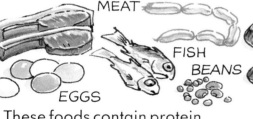

MEAT

FISH

BEANS

EGGS

These foods contain protein. Proteins are the main body building foods and you need to eat a lot when you are growing.

You need protein, even when you are fully grown, because parts of your body wear out and need to be replaced.

When you rub yourself dry after a bath, you sometimes rub off dead skin. Dead skin is old skin cells. The protein you eat helps to build up new skin cells.

MILK

YOGHURT

CHEESE

These foods contain calcium which helps to make your bones and teeth strong. They also contain protein.

PASTA

RICE

BREAD

SUGAR

These foods are called carbohydrates. They give you most of your energy.

Soldiers and mountaineers usually carry a bar of chocolate for instant energy.

VEGETABLES

FRUIT

Fruits and vegetables contain some of the vitamins and minerals your body needs to keep it in good condition.

The cellulose, which your body cannot digest, makes the food your body cannot use bulky so that your muscles have something to push against when you go to the toilet.

OIL

MAYONNAISE

BUTTER

MARGARINE

Fats also give you energy and your body can use them as a store of emergency food.

Stored fat helps to keep you warm in cold weather.

APPLE

MILK

BREAD

BUTTER

POTATOES

GREEN BEANS

MEAT

Try to plan a meal, like the one here, using foods on this page or others you think of. It should contain everything you need to keep healthy.

55

Moving skeletons

Look around at living things. You will find that they all have a particular kind of shape.

Animals, such as cats, dogs, birds and you, have skeletons either on the inside or outside which give them shape.

Try making a giraffe out of plasticine. Can it stand up?

Your giraffe collapses because it has no frame, or skeleton, to support its body. If you put plastic drinking straws in its legs and neck it will stand up.

STRAWS

How do you move?

Your skeleton is inside your body. It is made up of over 200 bones which are joined by tough fibres, called ligaments. The place where two bones meet is called a joint.

Your hips and shoulders have ball and socket joints so that you can move your legs and arms in most directions.

The lower part of your arm has two bones joined to your wrist bones. These make a pivot joint so that you can turn your hands over.

Your skull is made of bones which are fixed together and make a helmet of bone to protect your brain.

The ribs in your chest form a cage which protects your heart and lungs.

Your elbow joint works like a door hinge and can only move up and down.

Without joints you would not be able to bend or move. Your arms and legs are moved by muscles pulling on bones on either side of the joints.

Try to match some of the bones you can feel in your body with this skeleton.

Watch your muscles working

Hold one of your arms out straight and put your other hand just above the elbow, as shown in the picture.

BICEPS

Lift up the lower part of your arm. You will feel a muscle above your elbow, called the biceps, getting fat as it contracts.

The biceps becomes short as well as fat when it contracts and this pulls up the lower part of your arm.

When you lower your arm again, muscles at the back contract. The biceps is long and thin when your arm is straight.

Muscle strength

The more you use your muscles, the stronger they become.

Ask a friend to press his hands tightly together. Try to pull them apart by gripping each wrist and pulling outwards, as in the picture.

You will find it almost impossible to pull his hands apart because you do not use these muscles very often.

PULL

Try again by crossing your hands over and pushing his hands apart.

It is easy because you use pushing muscles often and they are strong.

PUSH

Outside skeletons

Insects, spiders, centipedes, millipedes and shellfish, such as crabs, all have their skeletons on the outside.

LADYBIRD

WOODLOUSE

CRAB   PRAWN

If you look closely at a ladybird or a woodlouse, you will find that the outside of its body is hard. This is because its skeleton, called the cuticle, is on the outside.

Its muscles are inside its body and limbs and are attached to the cuticle.

An outside skeleton gives these animals good protection against enemies.

PILL WOOD-LOUSE

If you touch a pill woodlouse it curls up and its whole body becomes a hard ball.

Animals without skeletons

Muscles cannot work unless they have something to push and pull against. Worms, caterpillars, slugs and snails have no skeleton, so how do they move?

The bodies of worms and caterpillars are supported by water pressure in their cells. Muscles use the edge of these cells to push and pull against.

The moving worm

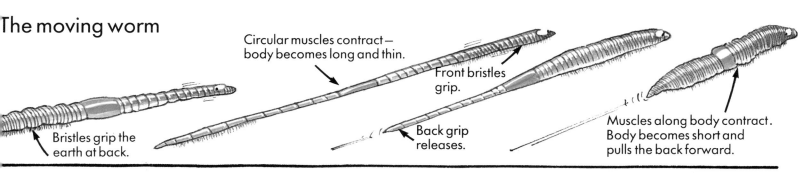

Circular muscles contract— body becomes long and thin.

Front bristles grip.

Bristles grip the earth at back.

Back grip releases.

Muscles along body contract. Body becomes short and pulls the back forward.

Slugs and snails

The bodies of slugs and snails are like one big muscular foot. This big muscle contracts and relaxes as it moves along.

You can see this happening if you put a slug or snail on to a sheet of glass and watch it moving from underneath.

FOOT

SNAIL

SLUG

SLIME TRAIL

The snail's shell is not a skeleton but it grows bigger with the snail.

The slimy trail it leaves behind comes from a gland at the front of its body. The slime smooths the way and helps to protect the slug or snail's body as it creeps over rough ground.

The snail can climb over a knife without being cut.

Unusual babies

Many baby animals, such as kittens and lambs, are exactly like their parents. But some babies, including caterpillars and tadpoles, look quite different from their parents. They go through a complete change, called metamorphosis, to become adults.

From caterpillars to butterflies

Butterflies mate early in spring, and the female then lays her tiny eggs on leaves.

EGGS

After a few days or weeks, tiny caterpillars hatch from the eggs. They eat part of the egg shell for their first meal, but soon move on to eat the leaves the eggs were laid on.

BUTTERFLIES MATING

CATERPILLAR HATCHES

The old skin splits and the caterpillar wriggles out in a new larger one.

Caterpillars spend their time eating and grow quickly. Their skins do not stretch and soon become too tight. They change their skins about four times as they grow.

Swimmers to hoppers

When the weather warms up in spring, male frogs go to their breeding ponds and sing in a croaky chorus to attract females. The male climbs on to the female's back, using special thumb-pads.

1

He is carried around on her back until the female frog lays her eggs, called spawn, which he then covers with sperms. The sperms swim through the egg jelly to fertilize the eggs.

SPAWN

2

3

TADPOLE HATCHES

About 10 days after the spawn is laid, little tadpoles wriggle out of the jelly. They have no mouths at first, and live on the remains of the yolk from their eggs. They breathe underwater through gills, feathery flaps on the sides of their bodies.

4

FEATHER LIKE GILLS

After a day or two, their mouths develop and they start to eat tiny water plants, called algae.

When the caterpillar is fully grown, a few weeks after hatching, it stops eating and moves to a hidden twig or leaf. The caterpillar spins silk from its body to hold it firmly on the plant. It then sheds its skin, and changes into a pupa.

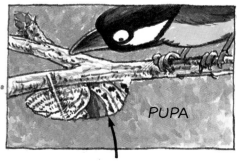

PUPA

The pupa becomes hard and looks like a broken twig or a bud, which helps to hide it from hungry birds. Inside, the caterpillar changes into a butterfly.

The gills are next to change. The tadpoles lose the gills on the outside and start to breathe with gills inside their bodies, like those of fishes.

5 BREATHES LIKE A FISH

When a tadpole is 6 to 7 weeks old, its legs begin to grow. First the back legs appear and then the front legs. At this stage it starts to eat small pond animals.

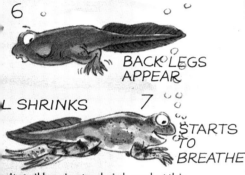

6 BACK LEGS APPEAR

L SHRINKS

7 STARTS TO BREATHE

Its tail begins to shrink and at this stage the tadpole comes to the surface to gulp air into its new lungs. It starts to hop out of the water — it is now a froglet.

8

Watch them grow

You can collect frog spawn from ponds in a jar, and watch tadpoles change into frogs at home.

Transfer the eggs into a dish at home and cover them with pond water.

Feed the tadpoles fresh pond plants until they grow legs, when they will need finely chopped raw meat.

Keep them in your home

Look for caterpillars in summer on grasses, nettles and cabbages. Gently place a caterpillar in a large glass jar with some of the plant you found it on.

PUNCH AIR HOLES

Cover the jar with some greaseproof paper held by an elastic band. Punch some breathing holes in the paper with a needle. Keep the jar in a cool place, and feed the caterpillar fresh leaves of the same plant each day.

If you have a cat, cover the dish with chicken wire to keep out playful paws.

When the tadpoles start gulping air, put a brick into the dish to make a landing stage. As soon as the froglets start jumping out of the water, it is time to take them back to their pond.

If you take caterpillars or tadpoles home, keep a record in your biology scrapbook of the changes you see.

If you are lucky, you will see the caterpillar change into a butterfly. Take the butterfly back to where you found the caterpillar and watch it fly away.

After two to three weeks the pupa skin splits and the adult butterfly pulls itself out.

At first its wings are wet and crumpled, but they stretch and dry after a couple of hours' rest.

The adult butterfly flies off to find food — nectar — a sugary substance from flowers. It also looks for a mate, and the life cycle starts again.

Take care of living things. Only take them home if you can look after them properly.

From seed to seed

Most flowering plants grow from seeds.

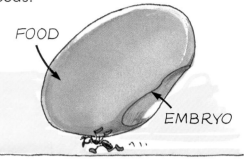

FOOD

EMBRYO

A seed is made of two parts, a food store and a baby plant, or embryo, which feeds on the food store.

The seed normally starts to grow in spring when the weather warms up and the soil is wet. The first part to grow is the root and then the shoot.

The seedling

The seedling lives off the food stored in its seed until it grows leaves. It then starts to make its own food by photosynthesis. It grows and produces flowers.

Sensitive roots

Roots are sensitive to gravity and always grow downwards.

Test a germinating bean to prove that this is true.

Soak a broad bean for 2 to 3 days, then pin it to a piece of cardboard or cork, resting on damp cotton wool. Prop the card upright and wait for the root to grow.

PLACE PIN THROUGH THE FOOD STORE.

CARDBOARD OR CORK, ABOUT 6 x 6 cm.

As the root grows, turn the board as shown. Each time you turn the board the root will turn to grow downwards.

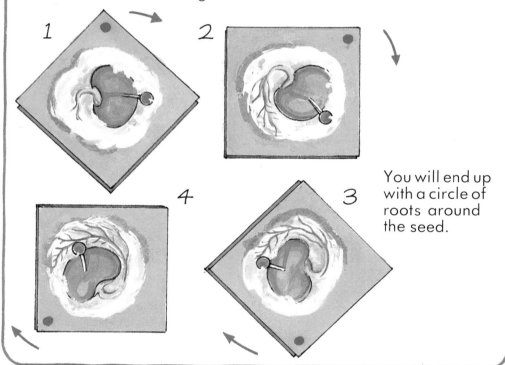

1 *2* *3* *4*

You will end up with a circle of roots around the seed.

Why do plants have flowers?

Flowers are the reproductive part of the plant. Without them plants could not produce seeds.

If you look closely at a buttercup or fuschia, you can see the male and female parts of the flower. Compare your flower with these pictures.

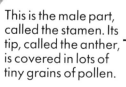

The ovary is the female part and is at the centre of the flower. The stigmas come out from the ovary and are easy to see.

BUTTERCUP

STIGMA

FUCHSIA

This is the male part, called the stamen. Its tip, called the anther, is covered in lots of tiny grains of pollen.

STAMENS

Before a flower can make new seeds, the stigma has to be fertilized by pollen. This is called pollination. The pollen usually comes from another plant of the same kind.

How does pollen travel?

Pollen is mainly carried from one plant to another by insects and the wind, but it is sometimes carried by birds, animals and water.

Pollen from the water lily is carried on the water to another flower.

Attracting insects

Flowers which are pollinated by insects usually produce sugary nectar to attract them. The plants also attract insects with their brightly coloured petals and sweet smells.

In spring and summer you can see bees, butterflies and other insects flying from flower to flower to feed on the nectar.

Try sucking the base of clover petals. The sweet taste is nectar.

CLOVER

While the insect eats, its body brushes against the stamen and pollen collects on its body.

When it visits another flower of the same kind, pollination will take place if the pollen brushes on to a ripe stigma.

Some petals have lines of colour leading to the centre of the flower to show the insect where to land.

PANSY

The broom flower has a special way of covering bees with pollen. When the bee lands, spring-like stamens flick up and cover the bee with pollen.

BROOM

You may have noticed that flowers, such as nicotiana and evening primrose smell strongly at night. This attracts moths to pollinate the flowers.

Blowing on the wind

Flowers which are pollinated by the wind need to produce lots of pollen to have a chance of reaching a stigma.

Try shaking a hazel catkin. The yellow dust that falls off is pollen.

This catkin is a male flower. The female catkin is feathery for catching pollen.

Grasses are wind pollinated. Pollen carried in the wind gives some people hayfever in summer.

Do wind pollinated flowers need to be colourful?

A new seed forms

When pollen lands on a stigma it grows a tube into the ovary to fertilize a female cell.

POLLEN

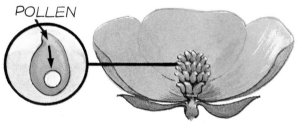

The petals wither and fall leaving ovaries, which are the fruit.

The seeds grow inside the fruits until they are ripe and ready to be scattered.

Travelling Seeds

All seeds grow inside fruits. Some of these fruits are the ones you eat, like apples and oranges, some are nuts, some are pods, some are berries and some are cones. Look carefully at the fruits and vegetables you eat and at plants growing in gardens and fields. You will see their seeds. Can you name the fruits around these pages?

When the fruit of a flowering plant is ripe, the seed or seeds in the fruit are scattered away from the parent plant. This gives some of them a better chance of finding the space, light and food they need to grow. Seeds are scattered in several different ways.

Hitch-hikers

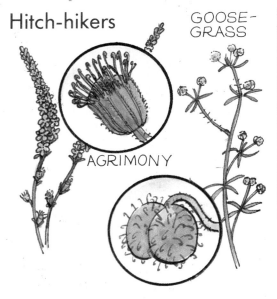

GOOSE-GRASS

AGRIMONY

Some seeds, such as burrs, "hitch" lifts from passing animals. The fruits are covered in lots of tiny hooks which can catch in the animal's fur. A burr can be carried a long way before it falls, or is scratched off.

15KM 10KM

You may catch burrs in your clothes.

Look closely at a burr. Can you see the tiny hooks?

Tasty fruits

Some seeds are inside soft, colourful fruits which are eaten by birds and animals.

The seeds are inside hard cases which pass out whole away from the parent plant in the droppings of the bird or animal.

Poppers

The pod is the fruit.

BEAN SEED

When seeds, such as beans, are fully grown, their pods burst open and flick the seeds away from the plant.

Under your feet

Some seeds fall to the ground and become sticky when wet. They stick to birds' and animals' feet and fall off again when they dry.

Try this experiment to see how many seeds you carry home after a summer country walk.

Fill a metal tray with soil.

Heat the soil in an oven to kill any seeds you may have dug up in the soil.

Scrape the mud from your shoes on to the soil, and water it well. Cover the tray with clear polythene and leave it in a warm place for 1 to 2 weeks. Do any seeds grow?

An unwelcome guest

Mistletoe grows on branches and trunks of trees. It sends its roots deep into the tree for water and minerals.

HOW DO SEEDS GET THERE?

Mistletoe seeds are very sticky. They stick to the bird's beak when it eats the berry. The bird later rubs its beak against a branch to wipe off the seeds.

The seeds lodge in the cracks of bark and, if conditions are right, another mistletoe will grow.

Ocean travellers

Coconuts may travel up to 2,000km on ocean currents before reaching land.

Fliers

Some seeds are blown by the wind to their new homes. Seeds which travel in this way normally have a special design which keeps them in the air for as long as possible.

Dandelion seeds are inside very small fruits, shaped like tiny parachutes. They can float on the wind for many miles before landing.

Blow a dandelion seed head. How far do the seeds go?

SEED

Another way seeds slow their fall from a tree is to spin like helicopter blades. You can make a paper model to see how this works.

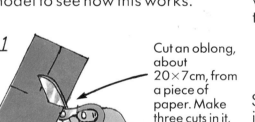

1

Cut an oblong, about 20×7cm, from a piece of paper. Make three cuts in it, as shown.

2   3

Fold over the two sides below the cuts, and bend the end up.

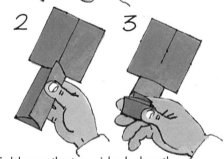

4

Fold out the two flaps at the top to make the blades.

Stand on a chair to drop your helicopter and watch it spin to the ground.

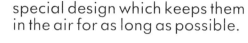

Sycamore seeds fall in this way, but they usually have only one blade.

SYCAMORE SEED

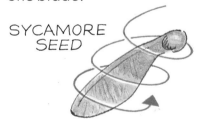

Cut off one of the blades from your paper helicopter. Does it still spin?

When you drop the one-bladed helicopter, you will find that it still spins. Try it out of doors and see how far it flies.

Trees

Trees are the largest living things on earth and they provide homes and food for many other plants and animals.

Is wood alive?

Snap a twig in half. Is it wet or dry? If the twig is alive, wet sap will ooze out.

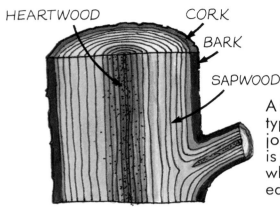

HEARTWOOD   CORK
BARK
SAPWOOD

A tree trunk is made of several types of wood and each has a job to do. The outside of the tree is protected by a layer of cork which is alive but its outside edge, bark, is dead.

Inside the cork is a layer of wood which carries starch from the leaves to all parts of the tree. Inside this, a new layer of wood, called sapwood is being made each year. Sapwood carries water and minerals from the roots to the rest of the tree. In the middle of the trunk is old sapwood, called heartwood, which is dead.

The heartwood supports the tree but it can live without it.

Bark rubbings

A tree's bark cracks, splits or peels as the tree grows and its pattern is different for each kind of tree.

Hold the paper steady, or tie it top and bottom.

Rub wax crayon firmly over paper.

Bark

Acorn

Oak Apple

Twig

Leaf

Oak Tree

Try making posters of different kinds of trees. Add twigs, fruits, flowers and leaf rubbings or prints. You can find out how to make prints on pages 76-77.

You can make bark rubbings, as shown above, and glue them on to a large sheet of paper to make a tree poster.

How tall is a tree?

You can work out how tall a tree is quite easily with a pencil and the help of a friend.

Hold pencil at arm's length.

Walk back until the pencil appears the same height as tree.

Turn the pencil on its side, bottom edge against tree.

STOP!

Ask a friend to walk away to one side of the tree, like this. Shout "stop" when she reaches the end of the pencil.

Measure from your friend to the tree with a tape measure. This distance is the height of the tree.

How old is a tree?

A tree makes a new ring of wood each year.

If you come across an old tree stump, you can find out how old the tree was by counting the number of rings.

Never carve your name on a tree. Disease may enter the wound and kill the tree.

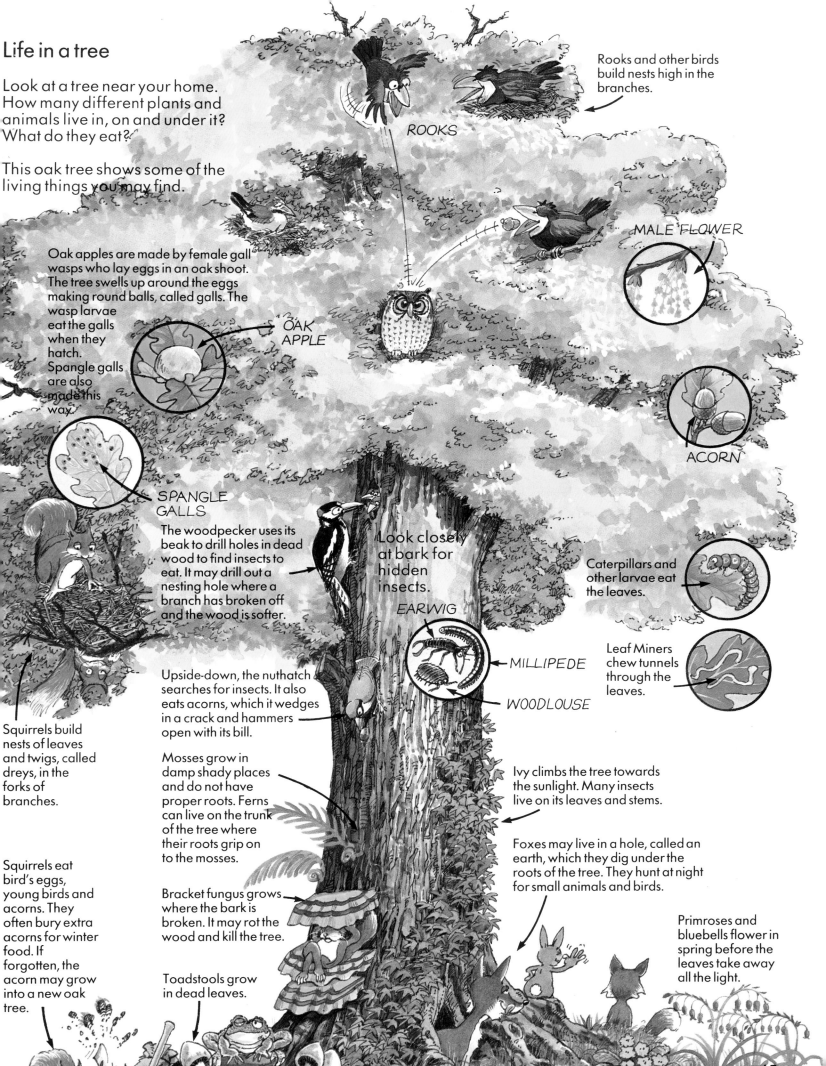

Life in a tree

Look at a tree near your home. How many different plants and animals live in, on and under it? What do they eat?

This oak tree shows some of the living things you may find.

Rooks and other birds build nests high in the branches.

ROOKS

MALE FLOWER

Oak apples are made by female gall wasps who lay eggs in an oak shoot. The tree swells up around the eggs making round balls, called galls. The wasp larvae eat the galls when they hatch. Spangle galls are also made this way.

OAK APPLE

ACORN

SPANGLE GALLS

The woodpecker uses its beak to drill holes in dead wood to find insects to eat. It may drill out a nesting hole where a branch has broken off and the wood is softer.

Look closely at bark for hidden insects.

EARWIG

Caterpillars and other larvae eat the leaves.

MILLIPEDE

WOODLOUSE

Leaf Miners chew tunnels through the leaves.

Upside-down, the nuthatch searches for insects. It also eats acorns, which it wedges in a crack and hammers open with its bill.

Squirrels build nests of leaves and twigs, called dreys, in the forks of branches.

Mosses grow in damp shady places and do not have proper roots. Ferns can live on the trunk of the tree where their roots grip on to the mosses.

Ivy climbs the tree towards the sunlight. Many insects live on its leaves and stems.

Foxes may live in a hole, called an earth, which they dig under the roots of the tree. They hunt at night for small animals and birds.

Squirrels eat bird's eggs, young birds and acorns. They often bury extra acorns for winter food. If forgotten, the acorn may grow into a new oak tree.

Bracket fungus grows where the bark is broken. It may rot the wood and kill the tree.

Toadstools grow in dead leaves.

Primroses and bluebells flower in spring before the leaves take away all the light.

65

Flight design

Wherever you are, you will see birds. They live in towns, in the country, on the seashore and even in deserts.

With the help of wings, birds can build nests and find food in many places that other animals cannot reach. See page 75 for ways of feeding birds at home.

Feathers

All birds have feathers and most, except birds such as ostriches and penguins, can fly. Feathers help birds to fly and keep them warm and waterproof.

Even the smallest hummingbird has about 1,000 feathers.

Feathers are made of the same material as your hair and nails, which is called keratin.

Soft, fluffy feathers, called down, keep the bird warm.

Like hair and nails, feathers can be soft or hard.

The outer wing and body feathers are stiff but very light.

Each little strand of the feather is joined by tiny overlapping hooks.

Cleaning and preening

STROKE UP TO TIP OF FEATHER

You can push the hooks apart with a finger. If you then stroke along the feather they will close again, like a zip.

Birds use their beaks to "zip" ruffled feathers together. This is called preening.

When a water bird preens, it usually spreads oil from a gland near its tail over the feathers to make them waterproof.

Birds need to keep their feathers clean and tidy to fly and keep warm. They often bath in water or dust before preening.

When oil is spilt from an oil tanker, many sea birds are covered with it. The heavy oil sticks their feathers together and they cannot fly. They try to clean themselves but they swallow the oil which poisons them and they die.

Using the air

Drop two pieces of paper, one crumpled and one flat, at the same time and from the same height. Which piece lands first?

The flat piece falls more slowly. This is because it has a larger area supported by the air than the paper ball. This is called air resistance.

When a bird's wings are stretched out to fly, they cover a large area. Air resistance helps to keep the bird in the air.

Bones are very heavy, but birds have hollow bones which help to make them light.

A wing is made of overlapping feathers joined to bones. When the wing flaps down, the feathers overlap and press against the air. When the wing comes up, muscles separate the feathers letting air through.

You can try this with water. Push your hands through it with your fingers together and then with them apart.

The greater push you feel when your fingers are together is like a wing as it flaps down.

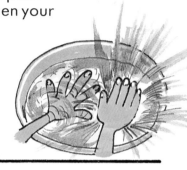

Designed for flying

A bird's wing has a curved, streamlined shape which is thicker at the front and thins down towards the back. This shape is

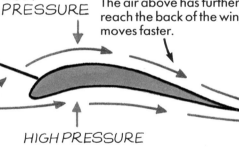

LOW PRESSURE

The air above has further to go to reach the back of the wing and so moves faster.

Air is pushed apart by the wing.

HIGH PRESSURE

called an aerofoil. When air meets the wing it moves in the way shown above.

Fast moving air has less pressure than slow or still air. This means that there is more air pressure below the wing than above and this pushes, or lifts, the wing upwards.

Try this test to show how air pressure works.

LOW PRESSURE

AIR PUSHES UP

Hold one end of a small strip of paper against your chin. Blow straight ahead. The paper lifts because the air pressure on top is less than the pressure underneath.

Take off

A bird's body has to be strong and very light to fly.

A bird needs speed for take off so that its wings will lift it into the air. Some run, others jump into the air and some push off from the water.

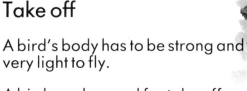

Birds nesting in trees and on cliffs take off by falling into the air.

A mallard pushes down hard with its webbed feet to leap up from the water.

A swan has heavy wings and needs to run quickly along the surface of the water, flapping hard, to take off.

Ponds and fishes

If you live near a pond, ask an adult to explore it with you and see how many different plants and animals you can find. A few of them are shown in this picture.

Be careful not to fall in!

Some insects, such as the pond-skater, can walk on the surface of the water without falling through.

The whirligig beetle spins about on the surface while it looks for food.

Holes in the bank could be the entrance to a shrew or vole's burrow.

You may see a water shrew or a water vole.

Make an underwater magnifying glass to watch the life under the water.

Cut the bottom off a large empty tin with a tin opener so that the tin is open at both ends.

BOTH ENDS OPEN

Cover one end with a clear plastic bag and tie it tightly with string so that it is waterproof.

If the water is clean there may be several different types of plant growing in the pond.

The water spider lives underwater in an air bubble.

The great silver beetle traps an air bubble in the hairs on its underside for breathing underwater.

The pond snail eats rotting plants.

The stickleback eats small pond animals.

When you put the tin on the pond, water will press against the plastic and bend it up. This makes the tin act like a magnifying glass.

Pond plants photosynthesize and give off oxygen into the water. Without them, oxygen breathing fish and other water animals would use up all the oxygen and die.

Why don't fish drown?

Fish, like all other animals, breathe in oxygen. How do they do this under water?

When a fish looks as if it is swallowing, it is forcing a mouthful of water over gills in the sides of its throat, and out through a flap. A fish normally has four gills on each side of its head.

The gills are a bony bar with lots of feather-like pieces called filaments. These filaments contain many tiny blood vessels. When water passes over them, the filaments draw in oxygen from the water.

Although there is more oxygen in air than in water, fish suffocate when they are out of the water.

FLAP CUT AWAY TO SHOW GILL BAR & FILAMENTS

Is shape important?

Water is 800 times denser than air. This is why it is much harder to walk through water than to walk on land. Fish need streamlined shapes to be able to swim quickly through the water.

WATER FLOWS EASILY PAST THE FISH

Which shape wins?

Cut out two small plastic boats from an old washing-up liquid bottle, like this.

Make one boat shaped and the other square, both with notches at the back, as shown.

Squeeze a blob of washing-up liquid over the notches. Put them in a bathful of water next to each other. Watch what happens.

The washing-up liquid acts like fuel to power the boats.

The square boat is slower because water cannot stream past it. The shape of real boats are copied from fish.

Expert swimmers

Fish have bendy spines which run along the whole length of their bodies.

Muscles pull on each side of a fish's spine in turn. This causes a wave-like movement to go down its body which pushes it through the water.

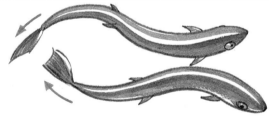

Its tail acts as both a paddle and rudder and its fins help it to balance, steer and stop.

If you put a small paintbrush in water, its bristles fluff out. When you take it out, they close up.

MAGNIFIED GILL FILAMENT

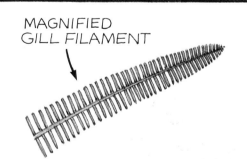

This is what happens to its gill filaments when a fish is taken out of the water. The filaments stick together and the blood vessels are less able to draw in air.

Upstairs, downstairs

A fish can float at different levels in the water by blowing up or letting down a bag of gas, called a swim bladder, under its spine.

SWIM BLADDER

Without a swim bladder, the fish would sink when it stopped swimming.

Submarines can float at all levels.

A submarine is built like a fish. It has ballast tanks which are filled with water to make it sink and are pumped full of air to make it float upwards.

What does a submarine's shape remind you of?

You can watch pond animals at home. See page 76 for details of how to make an aquarium.

Animal senses – 1

Sight, hearing, smell, taste and touch are all senses which tell you a lot about what is going on around you. Without them you would not know if you are hot or cold, comfortable or in danger. Your eyes are like cameras which take pictures of the world.

This picture shows you the parts of an eyeball.

OPTIC NERVE

IRIS

PUPIL RETINA

BLIND SPOT

RODS & CONES

Eyes need light to work. When you look at this book, light bounces off it and into your eye through the black hole in the middle, called the pupil.

The light touches special cells at the back of your eyeball and the information is sent to your brain by a nerve, called the optic nerve. Your brain then receives the information your eyes are taking

in. Too much light can damage these special cells. The coloured ring around your pupil, called the iris, closes up in bright light, making the pupil smaller. It opens up in dim light.

Watch your pupils close.

Look in a mirror in a dim room. Watch one eye and shine a torch into that eye. What happens to the size of the pupil? Does it change when you turn off the torch?

Why can't you see colour at night?

You have two types of cells at the back of your eye, called rods and cones. Cones only work in bright light and they pick up colours. In the dark there is not enough light

bouncing off things for the cones to work. You "see" instead with the rods which can work in dim light but do not pick up colour.

Night sight

Cats and other night hunters have mostly rod cells in their eyes. They can see much better in the dark than you can.

During the day, a cat's pupils are narrow slits but at night they open to catch as much light as possible.

DAY

NIGHT

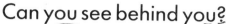

Do carrots help you see in the dark?

Your rod cells need vitamin A to keep healthy. Carrots contain carotene which is related to vitamin A. Healthy eyes are better at seeing in the dark.

Invisible colours

An evening primrose looks all one colour to you but it looks quite different to a bee. A bee's eyes can see another sort of light, called ultra violet light, which is invisible to you. Many flowers have markings which can be seen in ultra violet light and they guide bees to nectar at the centre of the flower.

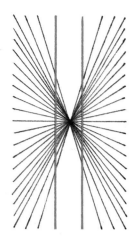

YOU SEE THIS

BEES SEE THIS

Can you see behind you?

Your eyes are on the front of your head but some animals, like rabbits and deer, have their eyes on the sides of their heads.

Look straight ahead with your arms behind your back. Bring your arms slowly forward until you can see both hands. The area in front of your two hands is called your "field of vision".

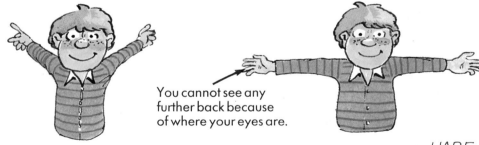

You cannot see any further back because of where your eyes are.

A hare can see behind as well as in front of its body because its eyes are on the side. This helps it to spot an enemy creeping up from behind.

HARE

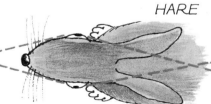

Animals with eyes on the sides of their heads see most things with one eye at a time. You see things with two eyes which helps you know exactly where they are. Prove this to yourself by trying this test.

Try touching the corner of a table with a pencil – it is easy. Then try to touch the same corner with one eye closed. Can you do it?

Hunting animals have eyes in the front for pouncing accurately.

Can you believe your eyes?

Are these two red lines straight? After looking at them, put a ruler against the lines to find out.

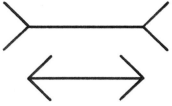

Which of these two lines is longer? Again, you can measure them after looking to find out the answer.

These tests help to show you that it is your brain which "sees" the pictures, rather than your eyes.

What is your blind spot?

Hold this page at arm's length, close your left eye. Look at the square and slowly bring it towards you. When the circle disappears you have found your blind spot.

Try again, closing your right eye and look at the circle instead of the square.

You have a blind spot in each eye where the optic nerve joins the retina and there are no rods and cones.

Animal senses – 2

How do you hear noises?

Throw a stone into a pond or lake and watch the waves spread out in bigger and bigger circles. Anything floating on the water will bob on the waves but will not move along. The waves move through the water but it stays still.

This is what happens to noises in the air. A noise makes waves in the air, called vibrations.

You can hear more clearly if you cup your hands behind your ears.

Your ears pick up the vibrations and send information about the noise to your brain.

Try talking to a friend about 30 strides away. Don't shout. Can he hear you? Try again using a homemade telephone like the one on this page.

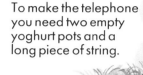

To make the telephone you need two empty yoghurt pots and a long piece of string.

Punch a hole in the bottom of each pot. Thread an end of the string into each pot and tie a knot to hold it.

Your friend can hear you now because vibrations from your voice are carried along the string to his yoghurt pot.

Try putting your fingers on the front of your neck when you talk in a deep voice. You can feel it vibrating. In your neck is your voice box and as it vibrates it makes a noise.

Where is the noise?

Many animals have ears which can move round to "face" a noise. Look at the donkey's ears in these pictures. First it hears one car. What happens when it hears two noises? If you have a cat or dog, you can see it prick up its ears when it hears something.

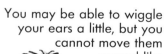

You may be able to wiggle your ears a little, but you cannot move them around like a donkey.

You know where a noise is coming from because you hear it in one ear before the other. You can test this with a friend.

Blindfold your friend and cover one of her ears. Tap a tin in front, behind and on each side of her. Does she know where you are? Try again with both of her ears uncovered. Is she more accurate this time?

Silent noises?

Some animals can hear sounds which you cannot hear. You can buy a "silent" whistle for your dog which makes a very high note. The dog hears it but you cannot.

Animals, such as barn owls, which hunt at night have much better hearing than you. They use their ears, as well as their eyes, to track down food in the dark.

Touch

When you pick up a pencil, you feel it because of cells in your skin which are sensitive to touch. These cells tell you about hot, cold, rough and smooth things.

If you put your hand on something sharp, the pain you feel makes you pull your hand away instantly. Pain acts like an alarm signal to warn your body when it is in danger.

Some parts of your body are more sensitive to touch than others. Try this test to find out where your sense of touch works best.

Ask a friend to close her eyes. Lightly press one matchstick and then two, held about ½cm apart, on her back. Can she tell whether there are one or two matchsticks? Try again on her wrist, arm and finger tips.

You will find that her finger tips are best at telling the difference. Why do you think they are more sensitive?

Whiskers

A cat's whiskers act like a fan of "feelers" around its head. At night it uses them to feel things in its way.

Smell

When you sniff, you draw smells up inside your nose where there are smell sensitive cells. These send information about the smell to your brain.

Smell can warn you that toast is burning or that food is bad as well as telling you that something delicious is cooking.

You may have noticed that you cannot taste food when you have a cold and a blocked nose. You taste with your tongue but your sense of taste is very weak without smell.

Many animals use smell to find food as well as for recognizing mates and enemies.

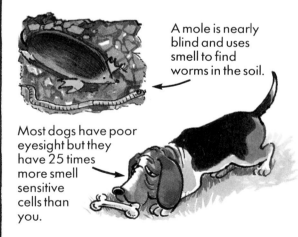

A mole is nearly blind and uses smell to find worms in the soil.

Most dogs have poor eyesight but they have 25 times more smell sensitive cells than you.

Insects do not have noses to smell with. Moths smell with their antennae. A male gypsy moth can smell a mate as far as 11km away.

A house fly tastes with its feet.

ANTENNAE

Attracting living things

Wherever you live, in the town or in the country, there are many ways of encouraging living things to visit you.

Wild patch

Most wild creatures do not like neat, tidy gardens. Ask your parents if you can have a corner of your garden to turn into a wild patch.

LONG GRASS

A pile of rotting wood can make a home for insects.

HONEYSUCKLE

BIRDS FEEDING ON INSECTS

COMPOST HEAP

NETTLES

Red admirals, peacocks and small tortoiseshells lay their eggs on stinging nettles. When the eggs hatch the caterpillars eat the nettle leaves.

In your wild patch, leave the grass to grow long and let nettles and wild flowers grow undisturbed.

This would be a good place to build a compost heap (see page 49). Birds will come to eat the insects that live in it.

If wild flowers do not grow in your patch, you can sow your own wild flower seeds. You can buy the seeds in a garden shop, or have fun collecting them for yourself.

DUG OVER PATCH

COW PARSLEY

POPPY

BUTTERCUP

DANDELIC

FORGET-ME-NOT

You can collect wild flower seeds throughout late spring and summer after the plants have flowered. Look for wild flowers on waste land in towns and on the edges of lanes and fields in the country.

Take a bag for your seeds and shake the heads of flowers into it.

Clear some small patches, about 30×30cm square, in your wild patch. Dig the soil over and plant the seeds about 1-2cm deep. Water them well.

The grass will soon grow again, and next spring and summer your wild patch should be full of wild flowers.

If you do not have a garden, you can plant wild flower seeds in a windowbox.

Make sure your box is safe and cannot fall off the ledge.

Butterfly guests

Butterflies will visit the wild flowers and nettles in your wild patch. They feed on flowers which have lots of nectar – you may have some in your garden.

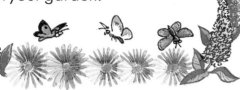

Homemade butterfly flower

You can make your own flower to attract butterflies.

Fill a small bottle with honey dissolved in water. Soak some cotton wool in the mixture and use it to plug the top. Fix the bottle to the top of a stick with elastic bands and push the bottom into the ground.

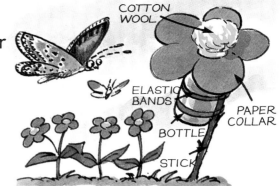

COTTON WOOL

ELASTIC BANDS

PAPER COLLAR

BOTTLE

STICK

A purple paper collar, held on with an elastic band, helps to attract butterflies.

Night visitors

If you put a light by a window on a summer night, several different kinds of moth will come to the window which you can watch from inside.

Window display

If you put food out on your windowsill, birds will soon come and eat, even if you are watching from inside.

Ask an adult to wedge a stick across the window. You can hang food from it as well as putting food on the sill.

Some food ideas:

Many supermarkets sell shelled nuts and fruit in net bags. You can fill an old net bag with nuts and tie it on to your stick.

Thread string through peanuts in their shells to hang up.

Make a small hole in the base of a yoghurt pot and thread some string through with a matchstick tied to the end to hold it. Fill the pot with a mixture of melted lard, breadcrumbs and currants. Let it harden before hanging up the pot.

Make a note of the different birds that come and the food that they like best.

PEANUTS

YOGHURT POT MIXTURE

NUTS

HALF COCONUT

Greenfinches, tits and sparrows will eat the hanging food.

Birds, such as blackbirds, will take food from the sill.

Bird bath

Birds need water to drink as well as for bathing.

You can make a very simple bird bath from a dustbin lid placed on bricks. Keep it topped up with clean water.

In winter, melt any ice with a kettle of hot water in the morning, or keep a night light burning under the lid.

If you have a cat, only attract birds to places out of its reach.

75

Collecting things

Keep a record of the things you see, as well as your experiments, in your biology scrapbook. You can add pressed flowers, leaf prints, sprays or rubbings, feathers and your drawings.

If you keep your scrapbook up-to-date, it will be an interesting record of living things throughout the year.

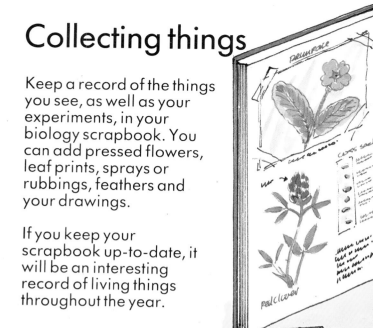

Pressing flowers

BLOTTING PAPER

Put the flower between two sheets of tissue or blotting paper in the pages of a thick book. Rest some heavy books on top. Leave it for about three weeks and then glue the pressed flower into your scrapbook.

An indoor pond

You can turn a glass tank into a lively pond at home.

Collect gravel from a stream or buy it in a pet shop. Clean it thoroughly in running water and then put it in the tank. Add some clean, hard stones to keep the gravel steady.

Ram's-horn snails are good "cleaners". They eat the green algae which grows at the side of the tank.

Keep sticklebacks in the tank. They eat water fleas and other small water animals. Buy some extra food from a pet shop to feed them.

In spring, the male stickleback's belly becomes bright red. He builds a nest. When he sees a female stickleback, fat with eggs, he does a zigzag dance to invite her to the nest and they mate.

DIVING BEETLE

ARROW-HEAD

STICKLEBACK

Collect or buy roundworms, flatworms, freshwater lice, shrimps, water fleas and water beetles.

FLATWORM

CANADIAN PONDWEED

WATER LOUSE

Slope the gravel forwards so that dirt collects at the front.

Pond animals need oxygen, so put in some Canadian pondweed and arrowhead. Push the roots or the bases of their stems into the gravel.

Cover the plants with a sheet of newspaper and gently fill the tank with clean water. The newspaper stops the water disturbing the gravel and plants. Take it out when the tank is full. Leave the tank for a week before adding animals. Do not stand it in the sunlight or too much algae will grow.

Leaf rubbings

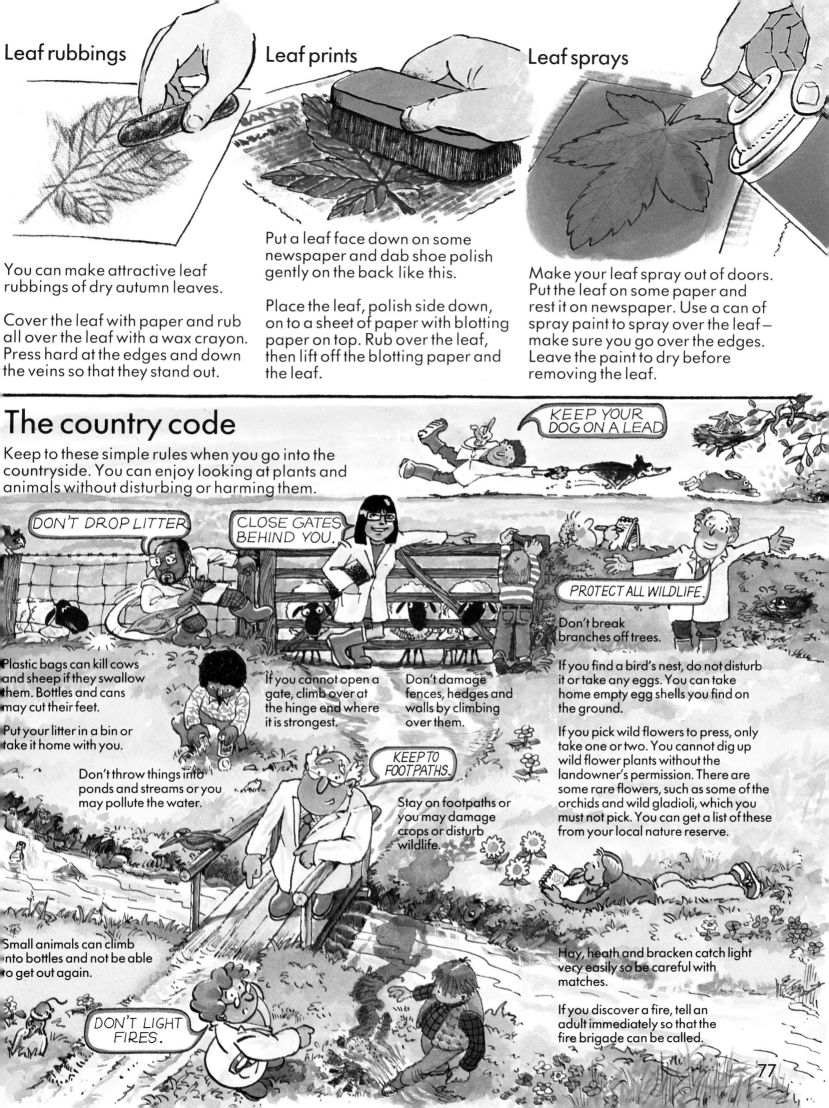

You can make attractive leaf rubbings of dry autumn leaves.

Cover the leaf with paper and rub all over the leaf with a wax crayon. Press hard at the edges and down the veins so that they stand out.

Leaf prints

Put a leaf face down on some newspaper and dab shoe polish gently on the back like this.

Place the leaf, polish side down, on to a sheet of paper with blotting paper on top. Rub over the leaf, then lift off the blotting paper and the leaf.

Leaf sprays

Make your leaf spray out of doors. Put the leaf on some paper and rest it on newspaper. Use a can of spray paint to spray over the leaf — make sure you go over the edges. Leave the paint to dry before removing the leaf.

The country code

Keep to these simple rules when you go into the countryside. You can enjoy looking at plants and animals without disturbing or harming them.

KEEP YOUR DOG ON A LEAD

DON'T DROP LITTER

CLOSE GATES BEHIND YOU.

PROTECT ALL WILDLIFE.

Plastic bags can kill cows and sheep if they swallow them. Bottles and cans may cut their feet.

Put your litter in a bin or take it home with you.

Don't throw things into ponds and streams or you may pollute the water.

If you cannot open a gate, climb over at the hinge end where it is strongest.

Don't damage fences, hedges and walls by climbing over them.

KEEP TO FOOTPATHS.

Stay on footpaths or you may damage crops or disturb wildlife.

Don't break branches off trees.

If you find a bird's nest, do not disturb it or take any eggs. You can take home empty egg shells you find on the ground.

If you pick wild flowers to press, only take one or two. You cannot dig up wild flower plants without the landowner's permission. There are some rare flowers, such as some of the orchids and wild gladioli, which you must not pick. You can get a list of these from your local nature reserve.

Small animals can climb into bottles and not be able to get out again.

DON'T LIGHT FIRES.

Hay, heath and bracken catch light very easily so be careful with matches.

If you discover a fire, tell an adult immediately so that the fire brigade can be called.

77

Glossary

carbon dioxide — This is a gas. When you breathe in air, your body uses the oxygen in the air and makes carbon dioxide which you breathe out. Plants take carbon dioxide from the air and use it for photosynthesis.

carnivore — An animal which eats only meat.

cellulose — The tough walls of plant cells, sometimes called fibre.

chlorophyll — The green chemical in the leaves and stems of plants which takes in energy from sunlight.

coniferous trees — Trees which keep their leaves during the winter. They lose a few leaves at a time throughout the year.

deciduous trees — Trees which lose all their leaves in autumn.

fertilization — When a male cell joins a female cell and a new animal or plant is made.

field of vision — The area you can see around you while you are looking straight ahead

germination — This is when a seed begins to grow. A seed needs warmth, water and oxygen to sprout.

gill — The organ a fish has on each side of its throat for breathing under water.

herbivore — An animal which eats only plants.

metamorphosis — The complete change some baby animals go through to become adults, e.g. tadpole to a frog.

nectar — The sugary liquid made by some flowers to attract insects.

omnivore — An animal which eats both meat and plants.

oxygen — A gas in the air which is used by your body when you breathe in. It is made by plants during photosynthesis.

photosynthesis — The way plants make sugar and starch from carbon dioxide, sunlight and water by using chlorophyll.

pollination — When pollen leaves one flower's stamen and is carried to the stigma of another flower.

senses — Sight, hearing, smell, touch and taste are all senses and their job is to tell your body about your surroundings.

swim bladder — A bag of gas under a fish's spine which it can blow up or let down to float at different levels in the water without any effort.

transpiration — This is when plants lose tiny, invisible droplets of water, mainly through their leaves, into the air.

warm-blooded — An animal who can keep the same body temperature whatever the temperature is around it.

Living Things Quiz

1 Does chlorophyll make leaves green, or keep swimming pools clean?

2 If you put a jar of pondweed in the sun you will see bubbles in the water. Are these bubbles of carbon dioxide or oxygen?

3 What will happen to seedlings if you put them in a dark cupboard?

4 Can you think of two reasons why plants need roots?

5 Do farmers add fertilizers to the soil because the plants like the smell, or because it improves the soil?

6 Gardeners sometimes keep a heap of rotten fruit, vegetables and grass cuttings to add to the soil. Is this called compost or manure?

7 About how much body heat is lost through your head; none at all, a quarter or half?

8 How do birds use their feathers to keep warm in winter?

9 Some animals sleep through the winter. Is this called dehydration, hibernation or transpiration?

10 What is the average body temperature of human beings?

11 Dogs cannot sweat, so how do they cool down when they are hot?

12 About how much of your body is made up of water; a quarter, a half or three-quarters?

13 Is a carnivore a plant-eater or a meat-eater?

14 Why do herbivores have flat, ridged teeth?

15 Which part of the food you eat helps make strong bones and teeth; carbohydrate, protein, calcium or fat?

16 The bones in your body are joined by tough fibres. Are these ligaments or joints?

17 Can you think of any animals that do not have a skeleton?

18 Are your biceps in your arms or legs?

19 Is metamorphosis something to do with a baby animal becoming an adult, or a seed starting to grow?

20 What is a baby frog called?

21 Which stage comes in between caterpillar and butterfly; pupil, moth or pupa?

22 Is the stamen the male or female part of a flower?

23 Some flowers are brightly coloured. Is this to attract the bees, or to make sure people see them and don't tread on them?

24 A coconut is a very large seed. How does it travel to find a place to grow; through the air, across the water or along the ground?

25 Are mistletoe berries sticky so that they can be used in glue-making, or so that they stick to birds' beaks?

26 Is the bark on trees dead or alive?

27 Is the fruit of an oak tree called an acorn or an oak apple?

28 How can you tell the age of a tree?

29 Are birds' feathers made of keratin, kerosene or carbohydrate?

30 Do waterbirds keep their feathers waterproof by swimming through oily water, or by spreading oil from a special part of their body over their feathers?

31 How are birds' bones different to humans' bones?

32 Which of these animals can walk on the surface of water; a water spider, a pond-skater or a great silver beetle?

33 What does a fish use its gills for?

34 What do fish use to help them float at different levels; a swim bladder, lungs or a rubber ring?

35 Are the pupils in your eyes larger in bright light or in dim light?

36 Can a hare see behind its body, without turning round?

37 Is the coloured part of your eye called the iris, the cones or the retina?

38 Noises make waves in the air. Are these called reflections, sensations or vibrations?

39 Which of your senses makes you feel that a thorn is sharp?

40 Which have a better sense of smell; dogs or humans?

Living Things Answers

1 Chlorophyll makes leaves green. (Chlorine keeps swimming pools clean.) See page 46.

2 The bubbles that you see in a jar of pondweed are bubbles of oxygen. See page 46.

3 Seedlings grown in a dark cupboard will be tall (because they are trying to find light) and yellow (because they need sunlight to produce chlorophyll). See page 47.

4 Plants need roots to anchor the plant in the ground and to take up water and minerals. See page 49.

5 Farmers add fertilizers because they improve the soil. See page 49.

6 Decayed fruit, vegetables and grass cuttings is called compost. (Manure is usually animal waste.) See page 49.

7 You lose about one quarter of your body heat through your head. See page 50.

8 Birds keep warm in winter by fluffing up their feathers to trap a layer of air. See page 50.

9 An animal's deep winter sleep is called hibernation. (Dehydration is when something dries out and transpiration is when plants lose water through tiny holes in their leaves.) See page 51.

10 The average body temperature of human beings is 37°C. See page 53.

11 Dogs cool down by panting. See page 53.

12 About three-quarters of your body is made up of water. See page 53.

13 A carnivore is a meat-eating animal. (A plant-eater is called a herbivore.) See page 54.

14 Herbivores have flat, ridged teeth to help them chew grass and hay. (Carnivores have long, sharp teeth to help them rip up meat.) See page 55.

15 Calcium helps make strong bones and teeth. (Carbohydrate gives you energy, protein helps you grow, and fat can be stored to keep you warm and to give you extra energy.) See page 55.

16 The tough fibres that join the bones in your body are called ligaments. (Joints are the places where two bones meet.) See page 56.

17 Worms, caterpillars, slugs and snails have no skeleton. See page 57.

18 Your biceps are in your arms. See page 56.

19 Metamorphosis is when a baby animal undergoes a complete change to become an adult. See page 58.

20 A baby frog is called a tadpole. See page 58.

21 Pupa is the stage between caterpillar and butterfly. See page 58.

22 The stamen is the male part of the plant. (The female part is called the stigma.) See page 60.

23 Some flowers are brightly coloured to attract the bees. See page 61.

24 Coconuts travel across water to find a place to grow. See page 63.

25 Mistletoe berries are sticky so that they stick to birds' beaks. See page 63.

26 The bark on trees is dead, but the cork layer just inside the bark is alive. See page 64.

27 The fruit on an oak tree is called an acorn. (An oak apple is made by the female gall wasp.) See pages 64-65.

28 You can tell the age of a tree that has been cut down by counting the number of rings. See page 64.

29 Birds' feathers are made of keratin. (Kerosene is another name for paraffin, and carbohydrate is a source of energy found in food.) See page 66.

30 Waterbirds keep their feathers waterproof by spreading oil over them from a gland near their tails. See page 66.

31 Unlike humans' bones, birds' bones are hollow. See page 67.

32 A pond-skater can walk on the surface of water, but water spiders and great silver beetles cannot. See page 68.

33 A fish uses its gills to breathe. See page 68.

34 Fish have a swim bladder to help them float at different levels. (Fish do not have lungs, and only humans need rubber rings!) See page 69.

35 Your pupils are larger in dim light than in bright light. See page 70.

36 Yes, a hare can see behind its body without turning round because its eyes are on the side, rather than on the front of its head. See page 71.

37 The coloured part of your eye is called the iris. (The retina is an area at the back of your eye and the cones are cells that are also at the back of your eye.) See page 70.

38 The waves in the air made by noises are called vibrations. See page 72.

39 Your sense of touch makes you feel that a thorn is sharp. See page 73.

40 Dogs have a better sense of smell than humans. See page 73.

HOW THINGS WORK

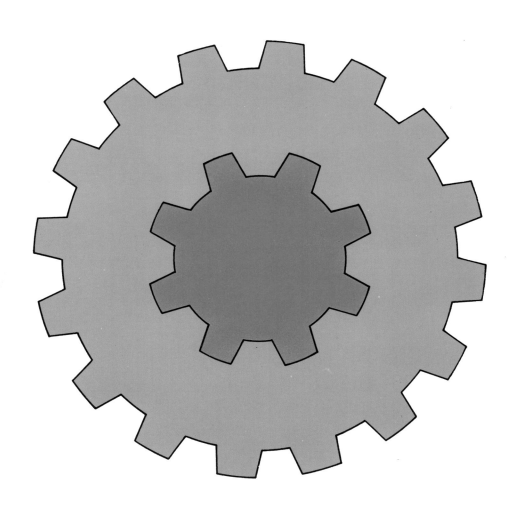

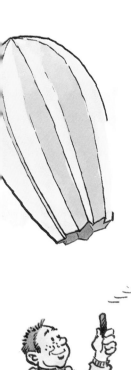

HOW THINGS WORK

Martyn Bramwell
Illustrated by David Mostyn
Designed by Sylvia Tate

Consultants: Alan Ward and Patrick Eve

Contents

Exploring science

The world is full of machines — from egg beaters and bicycle brakes to bulldozers and space rockets. Learning about how they work is great fun because they all depend on quite simple scientific ideas.

You can see these ideas in action for yourself by doing your own experiments and making working models. You will find that this book is full of interesting and surprising things to make and do.

Scientists are always asking questions and searching for the answers. You can do that too. Look around you and try to work out what makes things happen, in the world of nature as well as in

the world of man-made machines. Ask lots of questions, and try as many experiments as you can think of. Some work perfectly every time. Others are a bit more tricky. But remember that even the most famous scientists get things wrong sometimes. If an experiment does not work the first time, try it again. That is what scientific experiments are all about.

Home-made pulleys

You will need small pulleys for some of the experiments. You can buy them quite cheaply from most model shops. You can also make them yourself from cotton reels, old toy car wheels, or from cork and card.

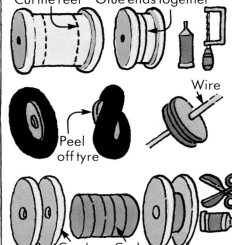

'Science corner'

All sorts of odds and ends can come in useful for experiments. Instead of throwing broken toys away, put any useful bits like wheels, springs, motors and fasteners into a box. You could keep another box for such things as plastic containers and bits of tubing, and another box for your tools, paints and glues.

Force measurers

In some experiments you will want to measure how much 'pull' it takes to make something happen. This is how to make a simple force measuring device.

You will need a fairly strong rubber band, two paper clips, a strip of sticky-backed paper, a bead, a short piece of string, some plasticine and a clear plastic tube. (The sort that toothbrushes are packed in work very well.)

Put the force measurer together like this. Then use the kitchen scales to measure out four lumps of plasticine weighing 100g, 200g, 300g, and 400g. (You will not need them again after the force measurer has been set up.)

PAPER CLIP HANGER

RUBBER BAND

BEAD MARKER

STRIP OF PAPER

STRING

PAPER CLIP HOOK

PLASTIC TUBE

Hang the force measurer up and put a mark on the paper strip opposite the bead. Now hang the 100g weight on the hook and mark the new position of the bead. Do this for each of the other test weights. You can complete the scale by adding extra marks at 25g intervals between the test marks.

25g marks

100g mark

No weight

100g weight

Now, if you attach the measurer to a weight and pull steadily, the position of the bead will show you how many grammes of 'pull' it takes to start the weight moving.

Weight

Good scientists are always **very** careful about safety, especially when doing experiments with sharp tools or anything hot. Take good care, and always ask a grown-up to help when you see this red warning colour.

What goes up usually comes down

When you throw a ball into the air it falls back to Earth. But what makes it do that? You used a force to send the ball up, so some other force must bring it back down. That force is called gravity.

Every object has its own force of gravity, from huge planets right down to atoms that are too small even to see. The bigger the object, the more powerful is its gravitational pull. And the closer you are to a big object, the more you can feel that pull. Earth's gravity is very strong. It keeps us all firmly on the ground. Without it we would float off into space.

The story says that Sir Isaac Newton discovered this invisible force when an apple fell on him from a tree.

The astronaut finds it quite hard to move about on Earth. His spacesuit and life-support backpack weigh as much as 26 kilos on Earth. This man's experiment pack weighs 12 kilos in Earth's gravity.

AIR SUPPLY
CONTROL PANEL

LIQUID FUEL TANK (700,000 KILOS OF FUEL)
BOOSTER ROCKET
REUSABLE SPACE SHUTTLE

Huge solid-fuel booster rockets and an enormous tank of liquid fuel for the second stage are needed to blast the two-million-kilo space shuttle far enough from Earth for it to escape Earth's gravity.

Which falls faster – a pebble or a paper tissue?

Drop an open tissue and a pebble from the same height. Which hits the ground first? Now try again with the tissue screwed into a tight little ball. What happens?

Gravity tries to make everything fall at the same speed. The open tissue slows down because it has a lot of air trapped under it.

Gravity power

A weight being pulled towards the Earth by gravity can be used as a source of power. Try making this simple model merry-go-round, driven by a falling weight. (When the model spins, watch what happens to the 'chairs'. We will come to this again later.)

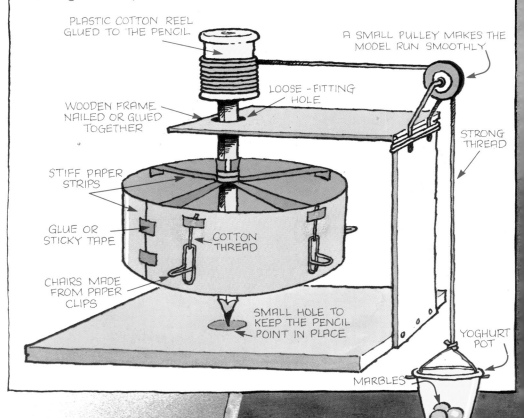

PLASTIC COTTON REEL GLUED TO THE PENCIL
A SMALL PULLEY MAKES THE MODEL RUN SMOOTHLY
WOODEN FRAME NAILED OR GLUED TOGETHER
LOOSE-FITTING HOLE
STIFF PAPER STRIPS
STRONG THREAD
GLUE OR STICKY TAPE
COTTON THREAD
CHAIRS MADE FROM PAPER CLIPS
SMALL HOLE TO KEEP THE PENCIL POINT IN PLACE
YOGHURT POT
MARBLES

As the astronauts travel away from Earth, the pull of Earth's gravity gets weaker. Far out in space it can hardly be felt at all. Being almost weightless when in space, the scientists float about.

Because the Moon is very much smaller than Earth, gravity there is much weaker. This crewman's experiment pack now weighs only 2 kilos, one-sixth of its weight on Earth.

SAFETY LINE

Outside the space-lab an astronaut drifts in a world where there is no 'up' or 'down'. How much do you think his experiment pack weighs now?

MOON BUGGY

Gravity at work

You can see gravity at work all around you. It can be used to do heavy jobs like breaking stones or driving posts into the ground. It makes liquids flow downhill without needing pumps. And a weight on a string always hangs straight down, so it can be used to check that things are perfectly upright.

The pile-driver keeps lifting and dropping a large weight to ram steel sheets into the ground.

The bricklayer uses a 'plumb-line' to check that his wall is not leaning.

The pull of gravity helps the joiner's hammer do its job.

Gravity makes the ready-mixed concrete flow down the chute.

Stopping and starting

Have you noticed how people standing on a bus lurch forward when the driver brakes, then sway backwards when the bus pulls away from the bus stop or traffic lights? It is all due to something called inertia. If an object is moving, inertia tries to keep it moving. This is why cars need plenty of room to stop. If an object is standing still, inertia tries to keep it still. That is why it takes so much pushing to move a broken-down car.

Stopping safely
In a car crash, the car stops very quickly but inertia tries to keep the passengers moving. Seat belts catch the passengers and stop them being thrown against the windscreen.

Fool your friends with inertia tricks

Question: Can you put the coin in the glass without touching either of them?

Question: Can you take the bottom coin away without moving the pile?

Do this trick in the garden using plastic picnic cups or unbreakable camping mugs and plates. Lay the table, put water in the cups, then see if you can whip the cloth away without spilling anything.

Answer: Flick the card sharply with your finger. Inertia keeps the coin still for the split second it takes for the card to fly clear.

Answer: Knock the bottom coin out of the pile with the blunt side of a kitchen knife. (A ruler will do if it is thinner than the coin.)

SNATCH THE CLOTH AWAY WITH A HARD LEVEL PULL.

The scientific detective
If you have one raw egg and one hard-boiled egg, you can use some simple science to tell which is which. Turn this into a game and challenge your friends to find the raw egg (*not* by dropping the eggs). Spin the eggs on a plate, then touch each one quickly with a finger but let go again at once. One egg will stop. The other will keep on spinning. That one is the raw egg. Can you work out why?

Inertia keeps the liquid inside the raw egg swirling round, and that starts the egg turning again.

Balancing

With a piece of thread, a pin and a weight you can find the balance – point of any flat cut-out shape. Hang the card and the weighted thread from the pin like this. Gravity will pull on the weight and make the string point straight down. Draw a line very carefully where the thread crosses the card. Hang the shape from another place on the card and draw a second line. The cut-out figure should balance exactly where the lines cross.

You could stick a picture on to stiff card and cut it out.

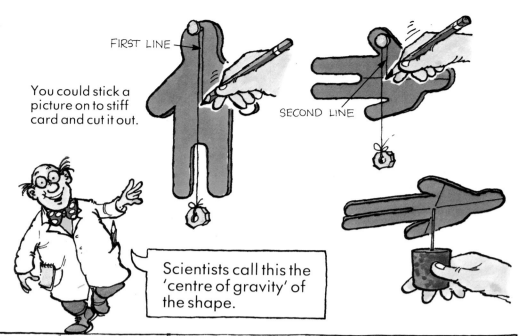

FIRST LINE

SECOND LINE

Scientists call this the 'centre of gravity' of the shape.

How far can it tilt?

Solid objects have a centre of gravity too. The lower down it is, the harder it is to tip the object over. That is why things like table lamps have a heavy base. See how far you can tilt an empty match box before it falls. Then try again with a rubber in the box, and finally with a heavy weight inside. Try a bolt with several nuts on it.

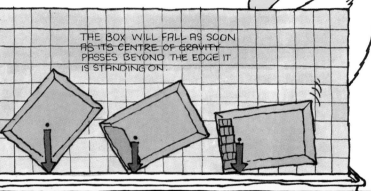

THE BOX WILL FALL AS SOON AS ITS CENTRE OF GRAVITY PASSES BEYOND THE EDGE IT IS STANDING ON.

Testing for safety

All the heavy parts of the bus are close to the ground so there is no danger of it tipping over.

The top deck is made from very light materials.

Engine, gearbox and other heavy parts are all low down.

The swing gauge shows how far the test platform is tilting.

Test platform

Hydraulic rams (see pages 106-107)

An 'impossible' balancing act

You can even make 'impossible' things balance if you cheat and change the centre of gravity. This model tightrope walker could never stand on the string without help. His centre of gravity is above the string and he would topple off. But if you hang a weight from his arms, that lowers the centre of gravity of the whole toy. Now it is below the tightrope and he is quite safe.

USE A SMALL CORK FOR THE HEAD

PIN THE HEAD TO THE BOX

BENT CARD GLUED TO THE BOX

TAPE

STRAW

TAPE

THIN STRING

Adding the plasticine brings the centre of gravity down here. The model's weight is now helping him stay on the string.

SPLIT THE STRAW AND GLUE TO PAPER FEET

STRAW

LUMP OF PLASTICINE

IF YOU SWING THE WEIGHT GENTLY, THE TIGHTROPE WALKER WILL WALK ALONG THE STRING

Magnifying muscles

Most simple machines, like levers, wedges and pulleys, work on the same idea. A small amount of 'effort' (the work you do) moves over quite a large distance. The machine then turns this into a bigger force moving only a short distance. This way, a machine can make a difficult or heavy job much easier.

Many of these simple machines have been used for thousands of years, but for most of that time they had to be worked by human muscles alone. Then water and wind power (pages 102-103) were harnessed to machines, and later still (in the last 300 years) steam engines, petrol engines and electric motors were invented.

More than 2,000 years ago the great Greek scientist Archimedes said, 'Give me somewhere to stand, and I will move the earth.'

What he said was quite true—at least in theory. But he would have needed a lever millions of kilometres long, *and* somewhere to rest the lever, *and* somewhere to stand way out in space!

Different levers for different jobs

Levers can be made to do different jobs depending on where you put the effort (that is, the work *you* do), the fulcrum (where the lever rocks or turns), and the load (the thing you want to move).

The longer your lever or crowbar is, the easier it will be to lift the rock.

Here the effort and the load are both at the same side of the fulcrum—but the lifting effort still has the longest lever.

This kind of lever magnifies movement. A small movement at the bottom of the rod makes the tip move a long way.

The chemist's weighing machine

This weighing machine works like the coin-and-ruler experiment on the opposite page. Your weight pulls on the short arm of a see-saw lever and this is balanced by a smaller weight working a much longer lever.

The counterweight balances the long arm at the other side so that the machine always starts off level.

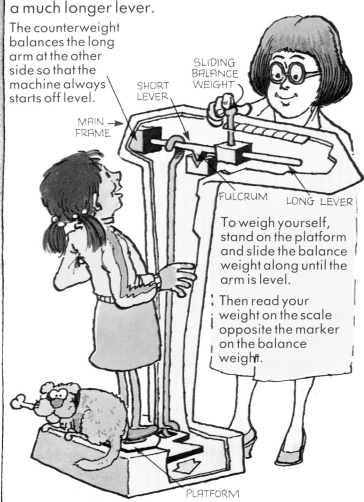

To weigh yourself, stand on the platform and slide the balance weight along until the arm is level.

Then read your weight on the scale opposite the marker on the balance weight.

How levers work

Put two coins on each end of a 20cm ruler and balance it across a pencil. Now try adding two more coins at one end. The ruler will still balance if you place these coins 5cm away from the pencil. This is because each side of the ruler is working as a lever, and two coins pressing on a 10cm lever give as much force as four coins pressing on a 5cm lever.

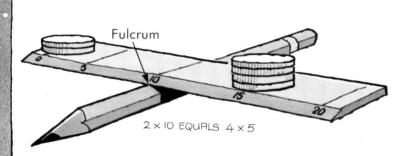

Fulcrum

2 × 10 EQUALS 4 × 5

You can experiment with levers using a plank. Here, the balance point (called the fulcrum) is at the centre and the plank is level, so Dad must be as heavy as Mum and Freddie added together.

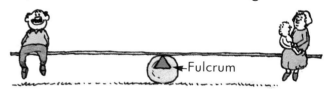

Fulcrum

This time Jenny has moved the fulcrum to give herself a very long lever. It has multiplied her weight so much that she can lift Dad right off the ground. She has made a lifting machine.

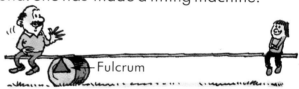

Fulcrum

Levers that write letters

Can you match any of the typewriter levers with the ones in the side panel?

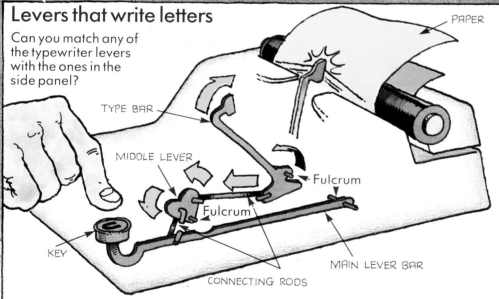

PAPER

TYPE BAR

MIDDLE LEVER

Fulcrum

Fulcrum

KEY

MAIN LEVER BAR

CONNECTING RODS

The mechanical typewriter is worked almost entirely by levers. When you strike a key, the main lever bar moves down and a connecting rod pulls the next lever. This gives a sharp pull to the bottom end of the final lever – the type bar – and this flies over and prints a letter on the page.

Launch-pad levers

This daring circus act is using a see-saw type of lever to send one member of the team flying high into the air. Why do you think the young boy was chosen for this trick? Would he go as high if just one adult jumped on the launching pad?

Fulcrum

Levers for lazybones

'Lazy-tongs' are simply chains of levers linked together. You could make some from the pieces of a construction kit, or simply from scrap wood.

Fulcrum

A couple of old teaspoons make handy 'grabbers'.

Slopes and screws

One of the simplest ways of moving a heavy weight is to drag it up a slope instead of trying to lift it straight up. The ancient Egyptians used this method when they built the great pyramids more than 4,500 years ago.

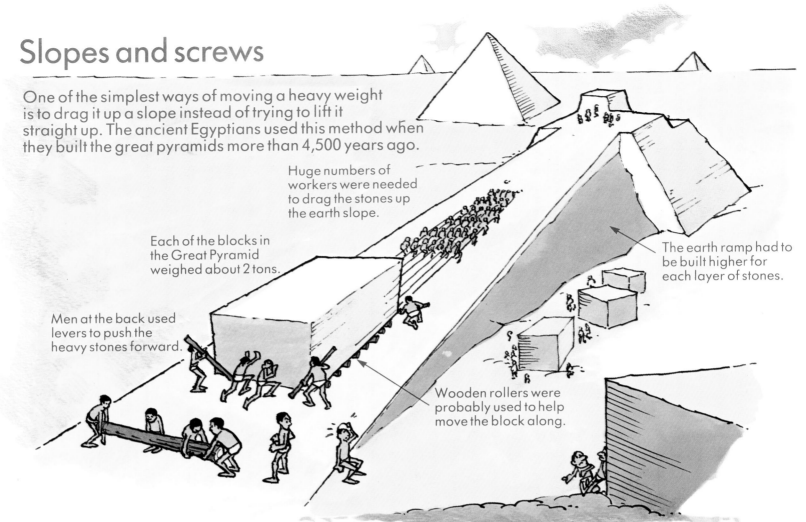

Huge numbers of workers were needed to drag the stones up the earth slope.

Each of the blocks in the Great Pyramid weighed about 2 tons.

The earth ramp had to be built higher for each layer of stones.

Men at the back used levers to push the heavy stones forward.

Wooden rollers were probably used to help move the block along.

Experiments with slopes

For these experiments you will need a force measurer. Page 85 tells you how to make one quite easily. Use your force measurer to see how much pull is needed to lift a toy lorry straight up from the floor.

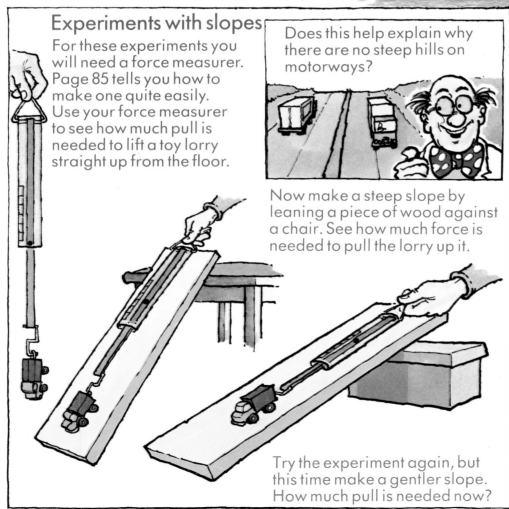

Does this help explain why there are no steep hills on motorways?

Now make a steep slope by leaning a piece of wood against a chair. See how much force is needed to pull the lorry up it.

Try the experiment again, but this time make a gentler slope. How much pull is needed now?

Using a wedge

A wedge works like two slopes stuck back to back. But instead of moving the load up the slope, you force the slope past the load. Here, the load is the log you want to split.

A blow with a hammer drives the wedge part way in. The wedge turns this into a much bigger force, pushing sideways to open up the split.

Rolling up a slope

If you walk up a hill on a spiral path it is much easier than going straight up. A screw works on the same idea. It is simply a long slope that has been 'rolled up' so it takes up less space. The more turns a screw has, the longer its 'path' is and the less effort it takes to move a load along it.

One turn of a piano stool with a gentle screw thread does not raise the seat far, but is easy to do.

A steep thread on the lifting screw raises the seat much more but it takes a lot more effort.

You can check the 'rolled up slope' idea like this. Cut out a paper slope and wind it on to a pencil. Then follow the edge of the paper with your finger.

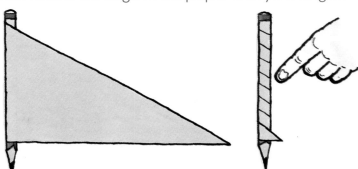

Screws with gently sloping threads move along slowly and take longer to do up, but they do not need as much effort as steep screw-threads.

Machines that use screws

You can use a vice to hold things steady as you work, or to squeeze a joint tightly while the glue is drying. When you turn the handle, the screw is pulled through the threaded hole in the fixed part of the vice and the movable jaw closes.

The wood-drilling bit uses two kinds of screws. A small 'leader' screw pulls the drill into the wood so the cutters can do their job. Then the wood chips slide up the spiral screw so they do not clog up the hole.

The handle, called a 'brace', is another wheel-and-axle machine like the ones on page 94.

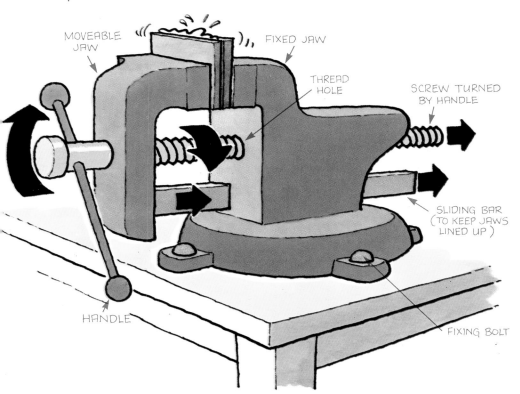

MOVEABLE JAW

FIXED JAW

THREAD HOLE

SCREW TURNED BY HANDLE

SLIDING BAR (TO KEEP JAWS LINED UP)

HANDLE

FIXING BOLT

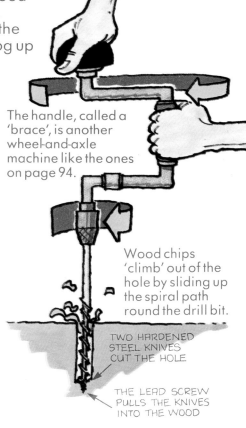

Wood chips 'climb' out of the hole by sliding up the spiral path round the drill bit.

TWO HARDENED STEEL KNIVES CUT THE HOLE

THE LEAD SCREW PULLS THE KNIVES INTO THE WOOD

Wheels, axles and pulleys

The wheel-and-axle idea has been used in machines for thousands of years. It works like a non-stop lever and, like an ordinary lever, it can turn a small force on the winding handle into a much more powerful force on the axle. This kind of machine is used in old-fashioned wells and in ships' capstans, but you can also see it in action turning a car steering wheel or working the pedals of a bicycle.

Drawing water from an old-fashioned well.

A neat safety device

The ratchet is a very useful little gadget. It allows the axle to turn one way, but when you stop winding the peg catches on the teeth and stops the axle spinning backwards.

Raising the anchor with a capstan turned by long levers.

The power of the pulley

In a pulley system, the force of the pull is spread right through the rope, so the more strands there are holding the weight up, the more the load is shared out.

Two pulleys will double your lifting power because the weight is being shared between two strands of rope.

Four pulleys, arranged like this, will give you four times as much lifting power.

Here is a good trick. The 2 kilogramme counterweight is helping you, so you only have to lift half the weight yourself.

4 KG PULL — 4 KG

2 KG PULL — 4 KG

1 KG PULL — 4 KG

2 KG PULL — 2 KG — 4 KG

One pulley is not much help. It only alters the direction of pull.

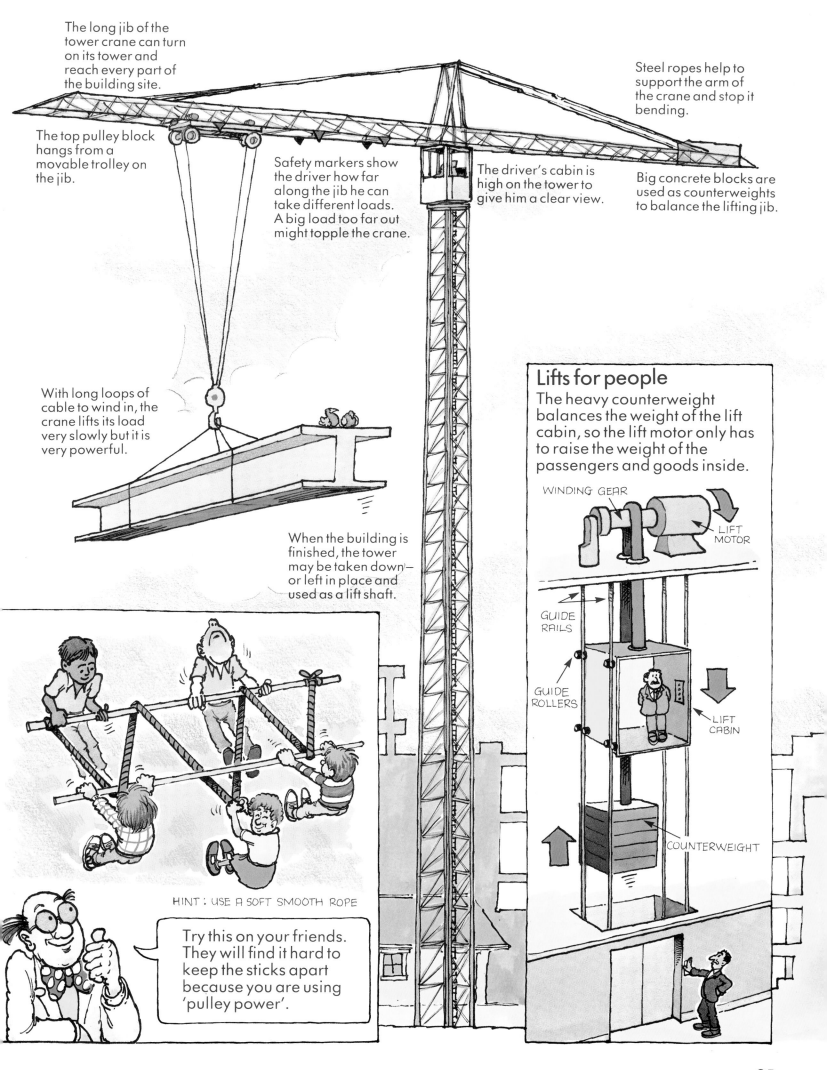

The long jib of the tower crane can turn on its tower and reach every part of the building site.

The top pulley block hangs from a movable trolley on the jib.

Safety markers show the driver how far along the jib he can take different loads. A big load too far out might topple the crane.

Steel ropes help to support the arm of the crane and stop it bending.

The driver's cabin is high on the tower to give him a clear view.

Big concrete blocks are used as counterweights to balance the lifting jib.

With long loops of cable to wind in, the crane lifts its load very slowly but it is very powerful.

When the building is finished, the tower may be taken down—or left in place and used as a lift shaft.

Lifts for people
The heavy counterweight balances the weight of the lift cabin, so the lift motor only has to raise the weight of the passengers and goods inside.

WINDING GEAR

LIFT MOTOR

GUIDE RAILS

GUIDE ROLLERS

LIFT CABIN

COUNTERWEIGHT

HINT : USE A SOFT SMOOTH ROPE

Try this on your friends. They will find it hard to keep the sticks apart because you are using 'pulley power'.

Sticking and slipping

What happens when you rub your hands together very quickly? They get warm. The force that causes this is called friction. It is a force that tries to stop things sliding past each other. Sometimes friction is very useful. Without it our feet would just slip when we tried to walk. It was probably the first way man found of making fire. And it is what makes car and bicycle brakes work. But there are also times when friction is a great nuisance. Engineers try to get rid of it in their machines because it makes moving parts get hot, and wears them out. It also wastes energy.

Spinning the stick very fast eventually makes the tinder (dry grass) start to smoulder.

The soldier sliding down a rope controls his speed by the friction between the rope and his clothing. But please don't try to copy him. It takes special training to do this safely.

Braking power

A bicycle brake uses the friction between a hard rubber pad and the metal rim of the wheel. When you squeeze the brake lever, another set of levers presses the pads against the rim and slows the wheel down. Feel the rim after braking hard; it will be warm.

Pincer levers

Brake pads

Unsticking sticky drawers

If you rub a soft lead pencil (such as HB or 2B) on a piece of paper and then rub your finger over the black mark, you will find that it is very slippery. You can use this tip to make a sticking drawer slide in and out smoothly.

Experimenting with friction forces

Use your force measurer to see how much pull it takes just to start a block of wood sliding along a board. Test again, first with some smooth shiny paper under the bottom of the block, then with sandpaper. Smooth surfaces slide easily, rough ones cause a lot of friction. You can also try rubbing the block with a candle or wax crayon, or put some oil on the board. What happens then?

SANDPAPER

OIL

Spinning free

Ball bearings or roller bearings are often used to make wheels spin easily on their axles. The bearings roll round the axle instead of rubbing against it, so there is much less friction. You can test the ball bearing idea by putting some marbles under a tin lid and rolling it across the floor.

Floating without friction

The hovercraft lifts itself clear of the ground on a cushion of air, so it has very little trouble with friction. Huge fans suck air in above deck and blow it out underneath the hovercraft where it is trapped by a rubber skirt. A big hovercraft like the SRN4 can carry 254 passengers and 30 cars.

The propellers drive the hovercraft forward, and can swivel on their mounts to steer left or right.

FLIGHT DECK

A yoghurt pot and a polystyrene food tray from a supermarket are all you need to make your own hovercraft.

YOGHURT POT WITH THE BOTTOM CUT OUT

MAKE THE HOLE WITH A TIN LID OR PASTRY CUTTER

PASSENGER DECK

TURBINE FANS KEEP THE SKIRT FULL OF AIR

Whirling around

Whenever you ride on a playground roundabout you can feel a force pressing you outwards. The faster you whirl round, the stronger the force becomes and the tighter you have to hold on. This outward force works on anything that is whirling around – and it can be very useful. It can be used to control machines, or to spin clothes dry, or even to provide artificial gravity for scientists working in space stations. Man-made satellites stay in orbit because the outward force caused by their whirling movement just balances the inward pull of Earth's gravity. As soon as they slow down, they fall back to Earth. You can show how this works with a simple experiment.

Whirling the water away

Automatic washing machines use the whirling force. At the end of the wash, most of the water is pumped out of the machine. Then the motor starts the drum spinning very fast. The soggy clothes are pressed hard against the inside of the drum – just like the people on the fairground 'Roundup'. The clothes can go no farther, but the water can. It gets spun out through the hundreds of holes in the surface of the drum.

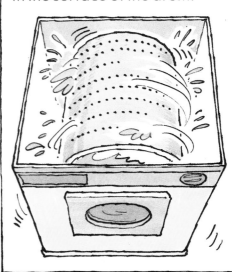

Satellites in orbit

Thread a length of fishing line or thin string through the case of an old ball-point pen. Then tie a paper clip very firmly to each end. Press a ball of plasticene weighing about 10g round one paper clip, and a larger ball weighing about 50g round the other paper clip.

ORBIT

10g 'SATELLITE' WEIGHT

FISHING LINE

PEN CASE

50g GRAVITY WEIGHT

BURY THE PAPER CLIP CROSSWAYS SO THAT IT WILL NOT BE PULLED OUT

Why doesn't the water fall out of the bucket?

Hold the pen-case upright and whirl the small 'satellite' round. Its outward pull will raise the big ball even though it is heavier.

Let the satellite slow down. As it slows, its pull gets less and the weight of the larger ball will put it back into a small orbit.

The same force holds the 'Death Spiral' car on its loop-the-loop track, even when it is upside-down.

Science at the fairground

Fairground rides and motorcycle stuntmen use the outward force of whirling objects to do things that look impossible.

The outward force presses the people against the wall of the 'Roundup' ride. They do not even have to hold on.

The faster the roundabout turns, the higher the chairs will fly. (Remember the experiment on page 86?)

The 'Wall of Death' rider can stay on the wall as long as he is going very fast.

Making gravity in space

Space stations of the future will spin like the sails of a windmill. The middle section will turn slowly, to allow supply ships to dock there, but the living areas and workshops at the ends of the arms will move quite fast.

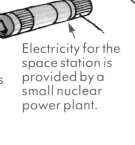

Spinning movement

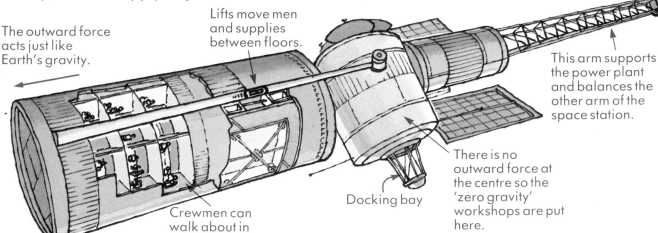

The outward force acts just like Earth's gravity.

Lifts move men and supplies between floors.

This arm supports the power plant and balances the other arm of the space station.

Electricity for the space station is provided by a small nuclear power plant.

There is no outward force at the centre so the 'zero gravity' workshops are put here.

Crewmen can walk about in artificial gravity.

Docking bay

Make a model space station

For the power unit, make a small hole in the base of a washing-up liquid bottle. Thread a thick rubber band through it. Anchor the band with a matchstick taped to the bottom of the bottle. Make a hook at the end of a piece of strong wire and catch hold of the band through the top of the bottle.

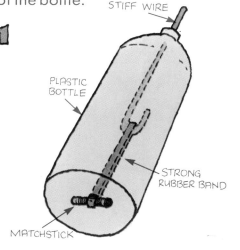

1 STIFF WIRE
PLASTIC BOTTLE
STRONG RUBBER BAND
MATCHSTICK

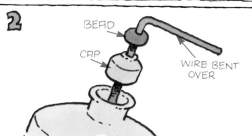

2 BEAD
CAP
WIRE BENT OVER

Cut the stopper off the bottle top and thread the top on to the wire. Add a small bead, then bend the wire over to one side.

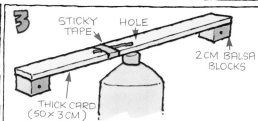

3 STICKY TAPE HOLE
2 CM BALSA BLOCKS
THICK CARD (50 × 3 CM)

Make the arm from a piece of thick card, 50cm × 3cm, and glue a small balsa block to each end. Fix the arm to the wire with tape.

4 HOLES
PLASTIC POT
WIRE WITH THE ENDS BENT OVER

Drill a small hole through each block. Make holes in two clear plastic food pots, then use stiff wire to hang them on the arms.

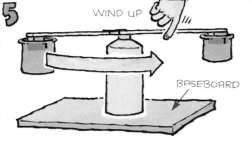

5 WIND UP
BASEBOARD

Glue the space station to a flat board to keep it steady. Then wind up the rubber band motor (about 50 turns) for a test spin.

6 Stand a plastic model spaceman in the pot. He should remain standing even when the space capsule swings out sideways.

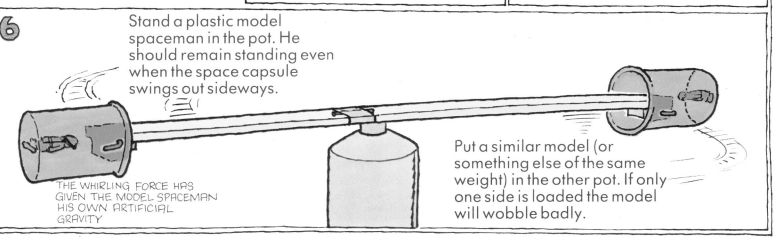

THE WHIRLING FORCE HAS GIVEN THE MODEL SPACEMAN HIS OWN ARTIFICIAL GRAVITY

Put a similar model (or something else of the same weight) in the other pot. If only one side is loaded the model will wobble badly.

Changing speed and direction

In any big complicated machine, all sorts of different moving parts will be in action at the same time. Some will be moving very quickly and others quite slowly. Some may be spinning round and round while others are bobbing up and down. One bit might be turning in one direction while the part next to it is turning the opposite way.

It would be very wasteful to have a separate motor driving each part, so large numbers of gears, belts, drive chains and connecting rods are used to take the power of the motor to different parts of the machine, and to alter its speed and direction once it gets there. Try spotting speed and direction changes in other machines in this book – like the typewriter (page 91), the lift (page 95), the windmill (page 102) and the steam engine (page 108).

Experimenting with home-made gears
Use the patterns on page 82 to make a set of gears like the ones below. For the experiments, fix your gears to a flat piece of wood with drawing pins through the centre. The teeth should interlock, but not tightly. Mark one tooth on each gear so you can follow it.

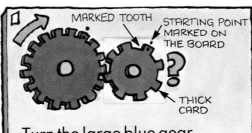

1. Turn the large blue gear through one complete turn. How many turns does the red gear make? And which way does it turn?

2. This time turn the small red gear through one complete turn. Watch what happens to the blue gear.

3. Now try it with three gears, two large ones and one small one. Make a full turn with the left-hand gear. What happens to the other two?

What controls the speed of the last gear in each row? (Hint: try counting teeth.)

Gears that tell the time
The energy stored in the main spring is released a little at a time by the escape wheel and lever. This energy is fed to the clock hands by a set of gears.

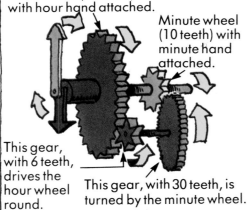

Hour wheel (24 teeth) with hour hand attached.

Minute wheel (10 teeth) with minute hand attached.

This gear, with 6 teeth, drives the hour wheel round.

This gear, with 30 teeth, is turned by the minute wheel.

The number of teeth on each gear wheel is carefully worked out so that the minute hand goes round 12 times in the same time it takes the hour hand to go round once.

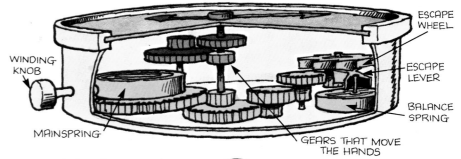

The six o'clock puzzle
Suppose we start with the hands like this, at six o'clock. We know how many teeth each wheel has, and we know that the two drive gears are fixed together, so if one makes a full turn, so does the other. Can you work out what time the clock will show when the drive gears have made one full turn?

It will show nine o'clock. The minute wheel will have made three turns, and the hour wheel will have made a quarter turn.

100

Driving, turning, bobbing and rocking

The car engine is a marvellous example of lots of moving parts all working together. Follow the action on the drawing. Petrol explodes in the cylinder and drives the piston down. The connecting rod turns the crankshaft and a toothed wheel at the far end moves a chain. This turns another wheel on the camshaft, and each time the pear-shaped cam comes round it lifts the push-rod. Finally the top of the push-rod works a rocking lever and this opens and shuts the valve to let in the next squirt of petrol.

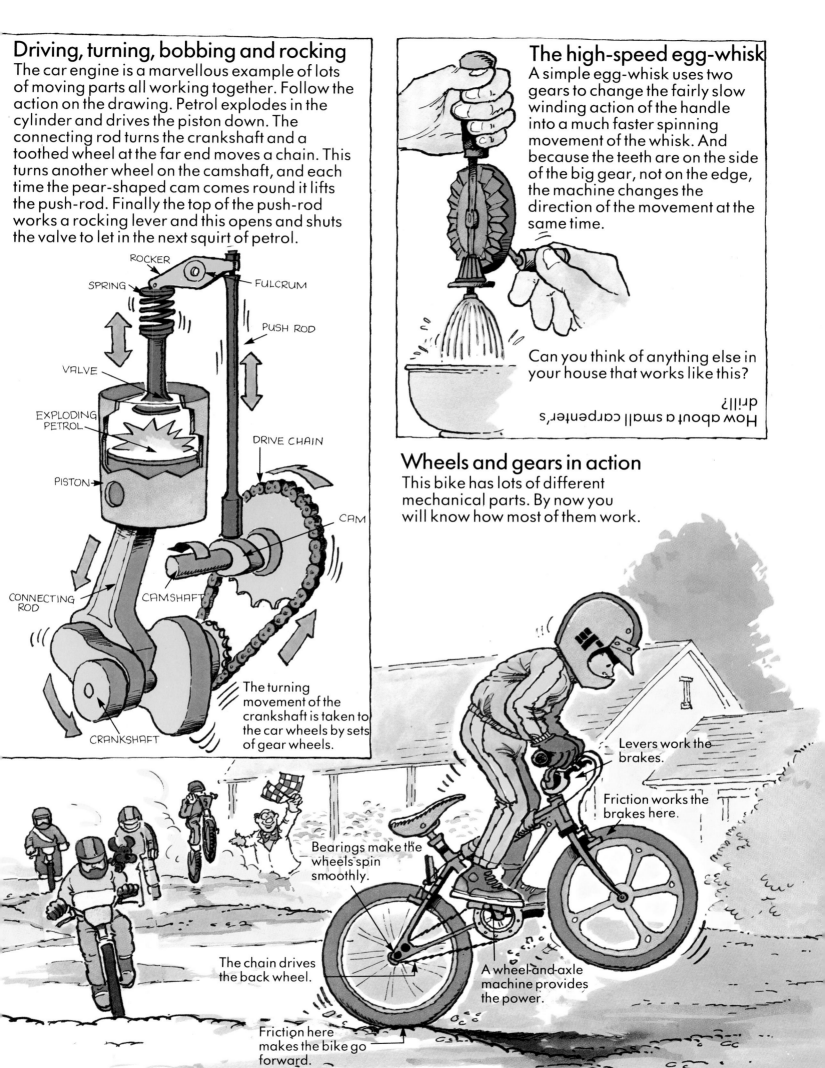

ROCKER

SPRING

FULCRUM

PUSH ROD

VALVE

EXPLODING PETROL

DRIVE CHAIN

PISTON

CAM

CONNECTING ROD

CAMSHAFT

CRANKSHAFT

The turning movement of the crankshaft is taken to the car wheels by sets of gear wheels.

The high-speed egg-whisk

A simple egg-whisk uses two gears to change the fairly slow winding action of the handle into a much faster spinning movement of the whisk. And because the teeth are on the side of the big gear, not on the edge, the machine changes the direction of the movement at the same time.

Can you think of anything else in your house that works like this?

How about a small carpenter's drill?

Wheels and gears in action

This bike has lots of different mechanical parts. By now you will know how most of them work.

Levers work the brakes.

Friction works the brakes here.

Bearings make the wheels spin smoothly.

The chain drives the back wheel.

A wheel-and-axle machine provides the power.

Friction here makes the bike go forward.

101

Power from nature

Water-mills have been used as a source of power for more than 2,000 years. At first they were used to power corn mills, but later they drove blacksmiths' forges, water pumps and weaving and spinning machines. They were easy to build, hardly ever broke down and cost nothing to run. Windmills have not been around for quite so long, but they too have been used all over the world for more than 1,000 years.

Nowadays, most of our machines are powered by electricity, made by power stations burning coal or expensive oil. Other machines, like cars and aeroplanes, burn petrol, diesel or aviation fuel, also made from oil. So engineers have started to look again at new ways of using cheap natural power – from the wind, the rivers, and even the ocean tides.

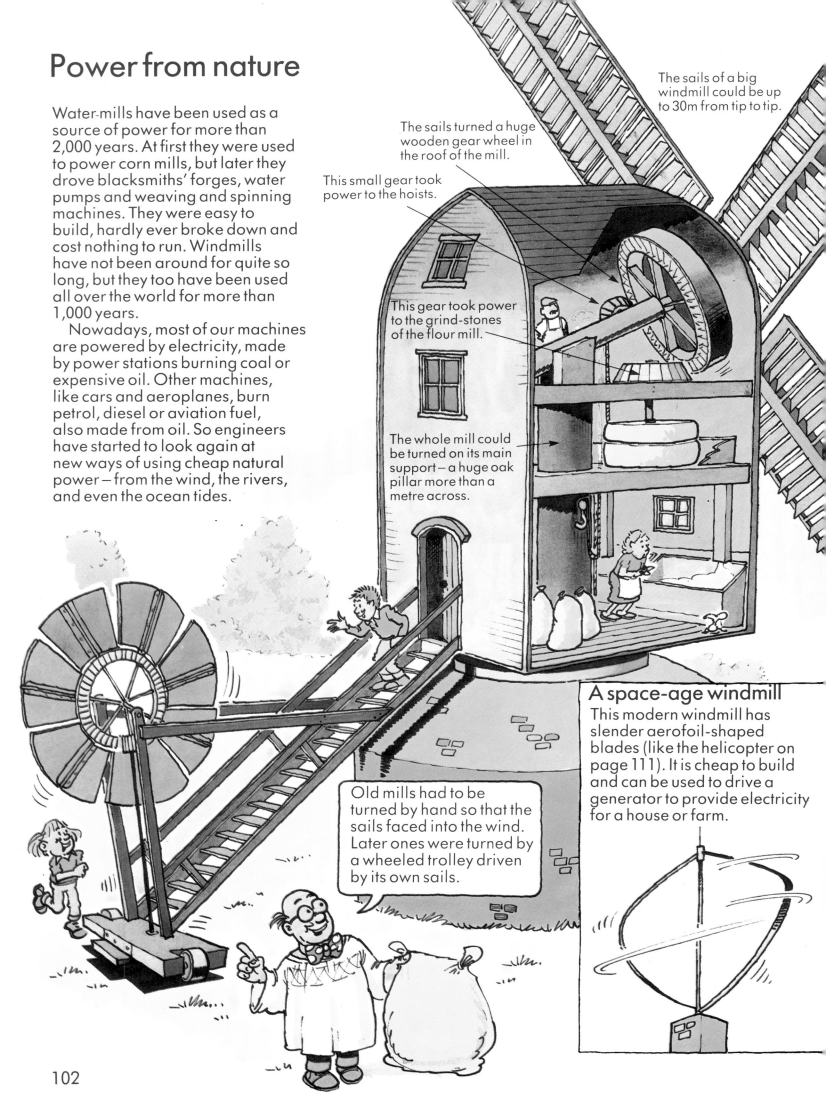

The sails of a big windmill could be up to 30m from tip to tip.

The sails turned a huge wooden gear wheel in the roof of the mill.

This small gear took power to the hoists.

This gear took power to the grind-stones of the flour mill.

The whole mill could be turned on its main support – a huge oak pillar more than a metre across.

Old mills had to be turned by hand so that the sails faced into the wind. Later ones were turned by a wheeled trolley driven by its own sails.

A space-age windmill
This modern windmill has slender aerofoil-shaped blades (like the helicopter on page 111). It is cheap to build and can be used to drive a generator to provide electricity for a house or farm.

A simple spinner

You can make a windmill quite easily from a square of stiff paper, a long pin, a bead and a stick. Draw lines from corner to corner, then cut half-way from the corner to the middle.

Bend each of the marked corners into the centre and push the pin through them. Slip a bead on to the pin then push it into the stick. See which way it spins. What could you do to make it spin the other way?

Can you believe your eyes?

Draw a robber on one side of a piece of card, and the prison bars on the other. Tape two long pins to the card like this, then blow the card to spin the robber straight into jail.

 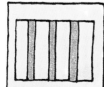

Water power at work

Next time you see a waterwheel see if you can work out how it was turned. Undershot wheels got all their power from the mill-stream pushing against the flat blades as it rushed underneath the wheel. Overshot wheels were turned partly by the force of the rushing water and partly by the weight of the water caught in the scoop-shaped blades. They made much better use of the power of the mill-stream.

Make your own water turbine

This kind of waterwheel is called a Pelton wheel. It uses a jet of water aimed at the spoon-shaped turbine blades. Can you guess what happens to the speed of the wheel as the bottle empties?

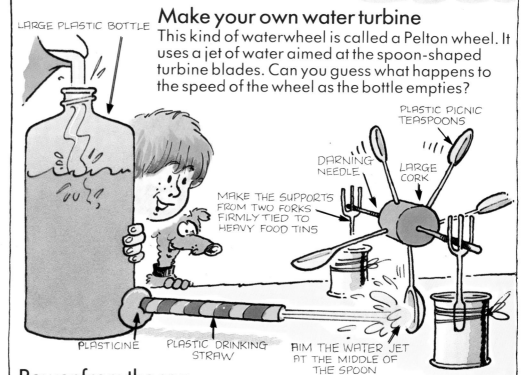

LARGE PLASTIC BOTTLE

PLASTIC PICNIC TEASPOONS

DARNING NEEDLE

LARGE CORK

MAKE THE SUPPORTS FROM TWO FORKS FIRMLY TIED TO HEAVY FOOD TINS

PLASTICINE

PLASTIC DRINKING STRAW

AIM THE WATER JET AT THE MIDDLE OF THE SPOON

Power from the sea

This tidal power station forms a dam across the mouth of a river on the coast of France. Its special turbines can spin in either direction, so electricity can be generated when the rising tide flows in from the sea through the turbine tunnels, and then again when the water trapped behind the dam is allowed to flood back out as the tide falls.

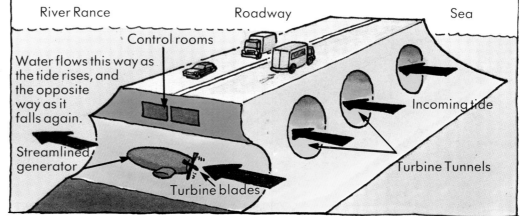

River Rance
Roadway
Sea
Control rooms
Water flows this way as the tide rises, and the opposite way as it falls again.
Incoming tide
Streamlined generator
Turbine blades
Turbine Tunnels

Putting on the pressure

It is very easy to think that air has no weight at all, but it has. The atmosphere presses down and around us, just as the water in the ocean presses on the hull of a submarine. Fortunately, our bodies are specially designed for life at the bottom of this 'ocean of air', and we do not even notice that more than a kilogram of air is pressing on every square centimetre of our skin. There are plenty of good experiments to show that air pressure is all around us.

AIR PRESSURE

INERTIA

Breaking the rule

Place a thin old wooden ruler on the table with about 8cm sticking over the edge. Then lay several sheets of newspaper over the ruler and smooth them out flat. Bring your fist down hard on the end of the ruler, and see what happens.

Did the newspaper fly up in the air as you might expect? If it didn't, what do you think held it down?

The invisible bottle-squasher
Very carefully pour some hot water into a plastic drinks bottle. Wait a few seconds for the steam to rise, then screw the top on tightly. Can you guess what will happen as the bottle cools down?

Rising steam pushes some of the air out.

The steam cools and turns back to water, leaving an empty space.

Now there is nothing to stop the outside air pressure squashing the bottle inwards.

No air can get in

Upside-down magic

Fill a tumbler with water, right to the brim, then lay a post-card across the top. Hold it in place and carefully turn the glass upside down. Take away the hand holding the card. Did your feet get wet?

BRIMFULL

WHAT IS HOLDING THE CARD IN PLACE?

Using air as a spring

If you squash air, or any other gas, into a smaller space, it pushes back. It is trying to spread out again and fill the space it used to have before you 'compressed' it. This pushing back is very useful. It makes the gas behave like a spring. If you block the end of a cycle pump with your finger, then push the handle in hard, you will feel the springiness of the compressed air inside the pump.

The 'hobby-horse' had solid wooden wheels and was a real bone-shaker.

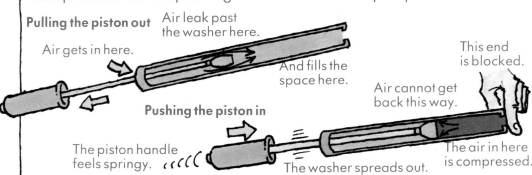

Pulling the piston out

Air leak past the washer here.

Air gets in here.

And fills the space here.

Pushing the piston in

The piston handle feels springy.

The washer spreads out.

This end is blocked.

Air cannot get back this way.

The air in here is compressed.

Modern bicycles have air-filled tyres that cushion the shocks.

How high can you go?

When you drink through a straw, all you really do is suck some of the air out of the straw. This makes the pressure inside the straw less than the pressure outside. It is the air pressing on the lemonade in the glass that pushes the drink up the straw to balance the pressure again.

The longest straw you could ever use would reach about 10 metres above the glass. That is as high as the air pressure could push your drink.

Air-pressure clues for weathermen

When the TV weatherman makes his forecast he often talks about the 'Highs' and 'Lows' on his chart. These are areas where the air pressure is higher or lower than normal, and they are good clues to the sort of weather we can expect. High pressure usually brings fine settled weather, but low pressure brings bad weather with blustery winds and rain.

THE TOP OF THE BOX CAN MOVE UP AND DOWN

THIS SIDE OF THE BOX IS FIXED TO THE CASE

THE SPRING STOPS THE BOX BEING SQUASHED FLAT

LEVERS THAT MOVE THE POINTER

Weather scientists (meteorologists) measure the air pressure with a barometer. Inside it is a metal box with nearly all the air taken out. High air pressure pushes the top of the box inwards, and a system of levers makes the pointer move round the dial. When the air pressure drops, the lid springs out again and the pointer moves the other way, warning of bad weather.

Big soft 'balloon' tyres can cope with very rough ground.

'Space-hopper' toys use the springiness of air compressed inside a strong rubber ball.

Some kinds of car shock absorbers work just like the cycle pump experiment. They have a piston inside that squashes a gas when the wheel hits a bump.

Heavy tankers and lorries have lots of wheels to spread their weight out.

Pumping and lifting

One of the big differences between gases and liquids is that liquids cannot be squashed. If you try the bicycle pump experiment on page 104, but fill the pump with water rather than air, you will not be able to compress the water at all. It will push back on the piston just as hard as you press in on the handle. This is a clue to another important group of machines. They are called hydraulic machines and they use liquids, usually a type of oil, to push pistons backwards and forwards inside cylinders. By using different sizes of cylinders the force can be magnified many times — to operate big, heavy machines.

Can water be compressed?

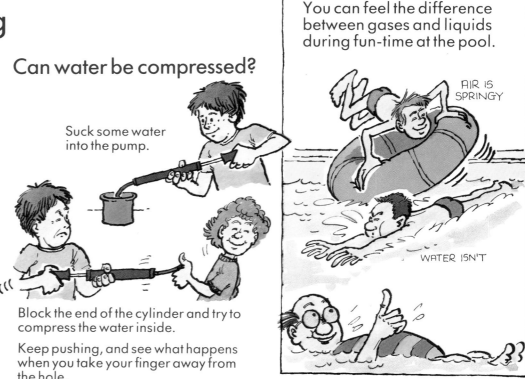

Suck some water into the pump.

Block the end of the cylinder and try to compress the water inside.

Keep pushing, and see what happens when you take your finger away from the hole.

You can feel the difference between gases and liquids during fun-time at the pool.

AIR IS SPRINGY

WATER ISN'T

Water-power

MAKE A SMALL GAP HERE SO THE AIR IN THE BOTTLE CAN GET OUT

Surprise your friends with this experiment. It proves the lifting power of water.

Fix a length of plastic tube or old garden hose into the neck of a hot-water bottle. (You may need a little help to get a watertight joint.) Then pile some heavy books on the bottle and carefully pour some water down the tube. You might expect the weight of the books to keep the bottle squashed flat, but to everyone's amazement it will fill with water and lift the books off the floor.

Lifting, pushing and squeezing with liquids

The great thing about trying to squash a liquid is that it pushes back with the same force in all directions. It makes no difference if the liquid is in a pipe with lots of bends, or in a square tank, or in a floppy bag like a hot-water bottle. The pressure spreads out evenly so that every square centimetre of the container has the same force pressing on it. This means that liquids can be used a bit like levers, to turn small forces into big ones. If the liquid is put inside two different-sized cylinders, joined by a pipe, a small force on the small piston will produce a much bigger force on the big piston.

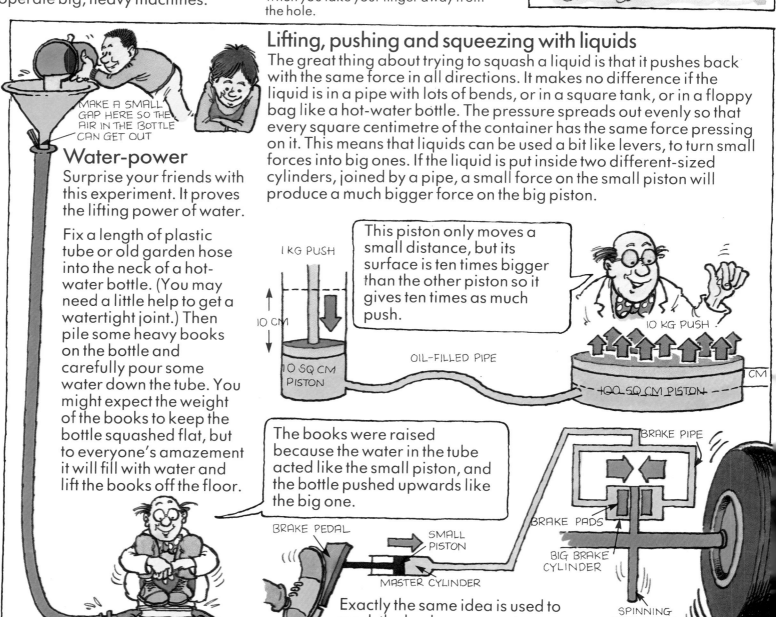

1 KG PUSH

10 CM

10 SQ CM PISTON

This piston only moves a small distance, but its surface is ten times bigger than the other piston so it gives ten times as much push.

OIL-FILLED PIPE

10 KG PUSH

100 SQ CM PISTON

The books were raised because the water in the tube acted like the small piston, and the bottle pushed upwards like the big one.

BRAKE PEDAL

SMALL PISTON

MASTER CYLINDER

BRAKE PIPE

BRAKE PADS

BIG BRAKE CYLINDER

SPINNING BRAKE DISC

Exactly the same idea is used to work the brakes on a motor car.

The village pump

The kind of pump you sometimes see on a village green is called a lift pump. A lever handle moves the piston inside the cylinder and simple valves, often made of flaps of leather, control the flow of water. Each time the handle is moved, one valve opens and the other closes. Water gushes from the spout each time the piston moves upwards. It is a bit like scooping up water with your hands.

The fireman's pump

This type is called a force pump. It squirts the water out much harder than a lift pump can. It has two valves as well, but they are both below the piston. The up-stroke of the piston fills the cylinder with water, then the downstroke forces it out through the pipe, like squirting water from between your hands. Firemen used pumps like this before powerful motor-driven pumps were invented.

The heavy brigade

If two-way valves are added to hydraulic cylinders, the pistons can be made to push in either direction (just like the steam-engine pistons on page 108). That is how powerful rams on a bulldozer can gently lift and lower the huge steel blade. See how many hydraulics you can find in this illustration.

The age of steam

Two hundred years ago, the world was a much quieter place. There were no engines, or cars, or big industrial cities. Machines were powered by people, or by windmills or water-wheels. But everything changed when the steam engine was invented. It could be big or small. It could be powered by burning coal or wood. And most important of all, it provided power wherever power was needed. Very soon, more people were living in cities than in the country. Huge factories were built to spin cotton and make cloth, and forge iron for bridges, ships and railways.

The early steam engine shown here used a coal-fired boiler to make steam. This was piped to the main cylinder where it forced a piston up and down. The piston was connected to a big wooden beam that rocked back and forth, turning the huge iron flywheel.

Any idea what this is? (Have a look at the opposite page.)

BEAM

CONNECTING ROD

CYLINDER

STEAM

GOVERNOR

FLYWHEEL

FURNACE

The spinning flywheel could be used to drive other machines.

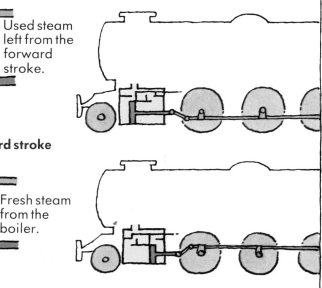

Steam inlet

Forward stroke

Steam outlet pipe

Sliding valve

Piston rod

Return stroke

Used steam left from the forward stroke.

Forward stroke

'Used' steam

Fresh steam from the boiler.

Getting the power to the wheels

The huge driving wheels of a steam locomotive are turned by connecting rods pushed backwards and forwards by pistons in the cylinders. A sliding valve lets steam in at one side of the piston to push it one way, then lets steam in at the other side to push it back again.

Engines for every job

Steam engines came in all shapes and sizes, from the small shunting engines used in marshalling yards to the 40-metre-long, 350-tonne 'Big Boy' locomotives used in the USA to pull long-distance goods trains at speeds up to 115kph.

The tender carried coal or wood for the fire, and water tanks to top up the boiler.

Automatic control

The steam engine's speed was controlled by a mechanism called a governor. Two heavy iron balls were spun round by the engine. If the machine ran too fast, the whirling force (page 98) made the balls fly upwards and pull levers to shut off the supply of steam.

If the engine runs too fast

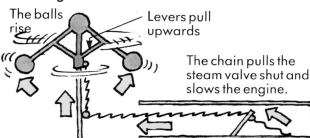

The balls rise

Levers pull upwards

The chain pulls the steam valve shut and slows the engine.

If the engine slows down

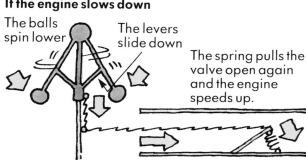

The balls spin lower

The levers slide down

The spring pulls the valve open again and the engine speeds up.

Believe it or not – it's a car. This weird-looking contraption was built in France in 1770. It was driven by steam and was the first real machine-powered road vehicle. It could travel at about 3kph.

Did you know . . . the world land-speed record was once held by a steam-driven car? The American 'Rocket' topped 200kph and broke the world record in 1906.

Steam-powered fairground traction engines were used to pull caravans, and were fitted with generators to make electricity for the fairground lights. You can still see them at fairs and country fetes.

Each 'chuff' of a steam engine is made by a blast of used steam from the cylinders being forced up the blast pipe. The draught sucks hot air from the firebox through the fire tubes and these heat the water in the main boiler.

Steam collects in the dome and is led from there to the cylinders by pipes running through the boiler.

CHIMNEY

SAFETY VALVE

USED STEAM FROM THE CYLINDERS

SMOKEBOX

FIRE TUBES FULL OF HOT GASES

BLAST PIPE

CONNECTING RODS

DRIVING WHEEL

CYLINDER

Up, up and away

If you hold a sheet of paper close to your bottom lip and blow across the top of it, you might expect it to be pushed downwards. But just the opposite happens. The paper rises, and stays up as long as you keep blowing. This gives a clue as to how birds and aeroplanes fly.

Whenever air rushes over a curved surface, like the upper surface of a wing, it speeds up. And the faster the air moves, the less it presses on the surface it is flowing over. With low pressure above the wing and higher pressure underneath, the wing is pushed upwards. Aero-engineers call this force 'lift'. It is caused simply by the air rushing over the wing, yet it can lift anything from a sparrow to a 400-tonne Jumbo jet.

BLOW ACROSS THE PAPER
FAST MOVING AIR = LOW PRESSURE
LIFT
STILL AIR = HIGHER PRESSURE

A working aerofoil

1 — 5CM — 8 CM — 7CM
2
3
4
5 THREAD
PIN HOLES
LIFT

Spot the aerofoils
Lots of natural and man-made flying things have the special aerofoil shape. See how many you can think of. (There are some clues at the bottom of the page.)

Take a piece of stiff paper 15cm × 5cm and make a fold 8cm from one end (1). Place the long side under a ruler (2) and pull gently upwards. This will give it a nice even curve (3). Tape the edges together (4) to make the special aerofoil shape. If you thread some cotton through holes in the wing, stretch it tight, then blow at the leading edge of the wing, you will be able to fly it up the thread.

Build and test-fly your own glider

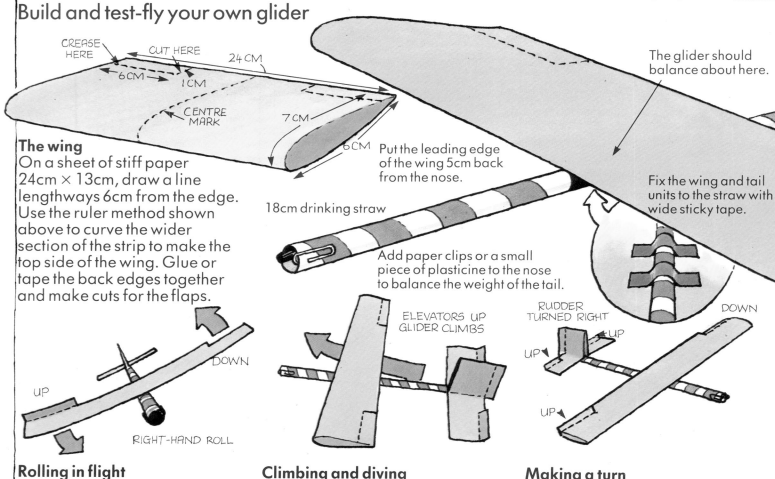

CREASE HERE
CUT HERE
6CM
1CM
24 CM
CENTRE MARK
7 CM
6CM
The glider should balance about here.

Put the leading edge of the wing 5cm back from the nose.

18cm drinking straw

Fix the wing and tail units to the straw with wide sticky tape.

Add paper clips or a small piece of plasticine to the nose to balance the weight of the tail.

The wing
On a sheet of stiff paper 24cm × 13cm, draw a line lengthways 6cm from the edge. Use the ruler method shown above to curve the wider section of the strip to make the top side of the wing. Glue or tape the back edges together and make cuts for the flaps.

UP
DOWN
RIGHT-HAND ROLL

ELEVATORS UP GLIDER CLIMBS

RUDDER TURNED RIGHT
UP
UP
DOWN
UP

Rolling in flight
You can make the glider roll in flight by moving the wing flaps (ailerons) like this. Always move one aileron up and the other down.

Climbing and diving
The tail-plane elevators are used to make the glider climb or dive. Unlike the ailerons, the elevators both move in the same direction.

Making a turn
A right-hand turn uses ailerons and rudder together like this. The elevators are turned up slightly to keep the glider's nose up.

A bird's wing-feather, a bird's wing, a boomerang, a sycamore seed, a Frizbee, a hang-glider.

Sailing into the wind

Old square-rigged sailing ships could only sail when the wind was behind them, pushing them along. But a modern yacht can sail in any direction, even into a head-wind. Does this bird's-eye view tell you how this is possible?

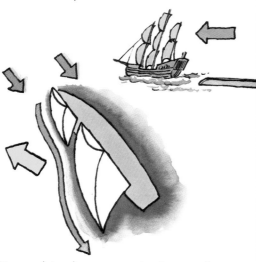

Does this shape remind you of anything?

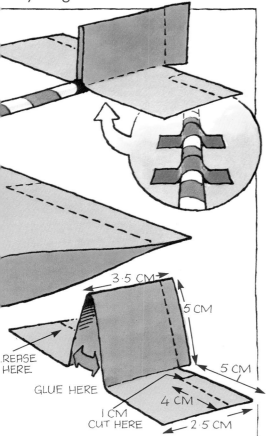

3·5 CM
5 CM
CREASE HERE
5 CM
GLUE HERE
4 CM
1 CM CUT HERE
2·5 CM

The tail

Take a piece of stiff paper 20cm × 3.5cm and fold it like this. Cut away the back 1cm of the tail planes so that the upright rudder is left sticking out. Make cuts for the elevator flaps and crease the paper along the dotted lines.

How helicopters fly

Instead of rushing along a runway to get enough lift for take-off, the helicopter stands still and makes its 'wings' rush through the air instead. The rotor blades are long narrow aerofoils, and the faster they spin, the more lift they make. The helicopter is steered by tilting the rotor unit in the direction you want to go. Because helicopters can hover, and land almost anywhere, they are used for rescue work and for lifting men on and off oil-rigs.

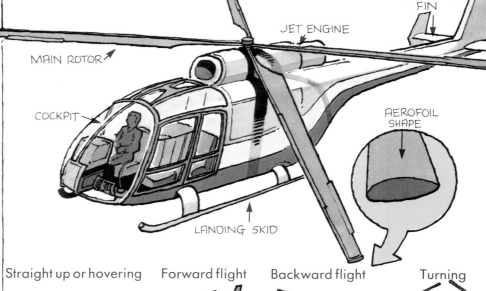

STABILISER FIN

JET ENGINE

MAIN ROTOR

COCKPIT

AEROFOIL SHAPE

LANDING SKID

Straight up or hovering   Forward flight   Backward flight   Turning

Hold your own helicopter championship

The drawings on page 116 show you how to make the main rotor for a model helicopter. All you need for your test flight is a pencil, and a fine day without too much wind. Wind your launching string round the bobbin, and slip the bobbin on to the pencil. Tilt the helicopter slightly in the direction you want to fly, then launch it with a smooth steady pull on the string. See how far and how high you can fly.

You can experiment by changing the amount of twist and droop on your rotor blades.

Heating up and cooling down

Whenever a solid object is heated it gets bigger. Scientists say it has 'expanded'. Some things expand more than others. Metals, for example, expand quite a lot when they are heated and this can cause problems for engineers. A big iron bridge like the Forth railway bridge is more than a metre longer on hot summer days than it is in winter when the metal is cool. Concrete bridges expand too, and if you look carefully at a motorway fly-over you will see there are small gaps in the road to leave room for the bridge to expand without causing damage.

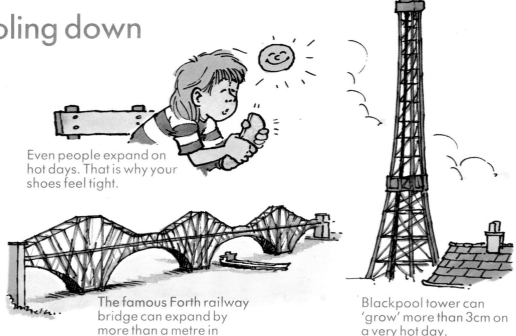

Even people expand on hot days. That is why your shoes feel tight.

The famous Forth railway bridge can expand by more than a metre in summer.

Blackpool tower can 'grow' more than 3cm on a very hot day.

The expanding rod experiment

This experiment is easy to do, but like all experiments that use flames it should only be done when there are grown-ups about. Set up the experiment like this and see how much a steel knitting needle expands. Try the experiment with rods of other metals. Do they expand by the same amount? If not, which metal expands the most?

Let everything cool down for 15 minutes after you have blown out the candles. The metal gets very hot.

The expanding rod rolls the needle along and the pointer magnifies the tiny movement so it is easier to see.

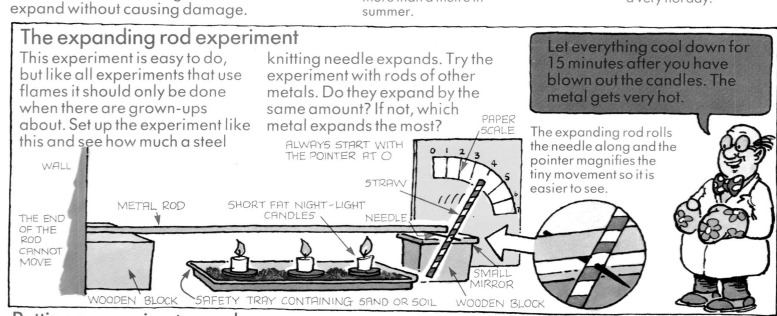

ALWAYS START WITH THE POINTER AT 0

PAPER SCALE

STRAW

NEEDLE

WALL

THE END OF THE ROD CANNOT MOVE

METAL ROD

SHORT FAT NIGHT-LIGHT CANDLES

SMALL MIRROR

WOODEN BLOCK

SAFETY TRAY CONTAINING SAND OR SOIL

WOODEN BLOCK

Putting expansion to work

If two strips, made of different metals, are joined together and then heated, the one that expands most will bend the strip into a curve. This can be used to turn an electrical circuit on and off. This kind of switch is used to control the temperature of an iron, and to control central heating systems.

Cold
The strip is straight

Hot
This side expands a little

This side expands more and bends the strip

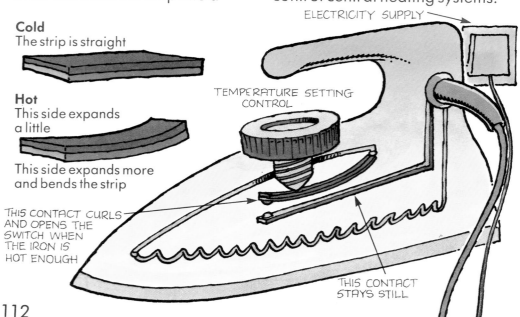

ELECTRICITY SUPPLY

TEMPERATURE SETTING CONTROL

THIS CONTACT CURLS AND OPENS THE SWITCH WHEN THE IRON IS HOT ENOUGH

THIS CONTACT STAYS STILL

A handy household tip

Next time your Mum or Dad cannot get the top off a jar, help them with simple science. Hold the jar top under the hot tap for a few seconds — then unscrew it (using a cloth).

Can you explain why the top comes off so easily?

Floating on air

Gases expand too when they get hot, and this makes them lighter so they float upwards. (You can test this by holding a piece of tissue over a hot radiator. The rising hot air makes the tissue flutter.) Page 117 shows you how to make a hot air balloon. Here is how to make the heater, and how to launch the balloon.

Hot air balloons work best on cold days when there is no wind. You could organise a balloon championship among your friends at school.

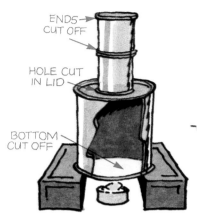

ENDS CUT OFF

HOLE CUT IN LID

BOTTOM CUT OFF

The heater chimney is made from a paint tin and two food tins. These need to be cut and joined together, so ask a grown-up to do this bit. Beware of sharp edges.

The heater is a small tin containing a wad of cotton wool soaked in methylated spirit (meths). Stand the chimney on some bricks, with the heater underneath.

Light the meths, then hold the balloon over the chimney but do not let it touch the hot metal. The balloon will fill with hot air until it is light enough to lift off.

Free hot water

Here is a good experiment for a hot summer day. Fill the hosepipe with water, turn off the tap, and leave the hose in the sun for a few hours. Then unfasten the tap connector and let the water in the pipe run into a basin.

Dark-coloured plastic pipes work best.

Test the water carefully. You will be surprised how hot it can get.

Keeping things cool

As you dry in the sun after a swim, the water on your body turns to vapour. But it needs heat to make the change – and it takes some of that heat from your body. That is why you feel cooler. Fridges work the same way. The pipes you see behind the fridge contain freon, a substance that can turn from a liquid to a vapour, and back again, very easily. Each time it changes it either takes in heat or gives out heat. Follow the freon round the pipes and see how it works.

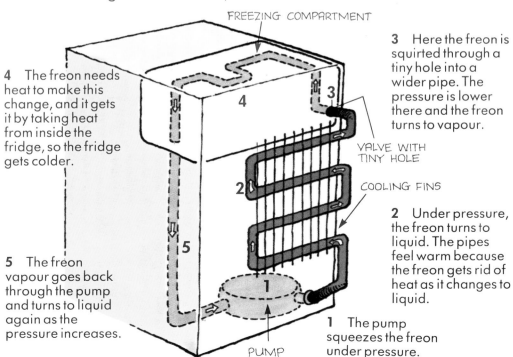

FREEZING COMPARTMENT

4 The freon needs heat to make this change, and it gets it by taking heat from inside the fridge, so the fridge gets colder.

3 Here the freon is squirted through a tiny hole into a wider pipe. The pressure is lower there and the freon turns to vapour.

VALVE WITH TINY HOLE

COOLING FINS

2 Under pressure, the freon turns to liquid. The pipes feel warm because the freon gets rid of heat as it changes to liquid.

5 The freon vapour goes back through the pump and turns to liquid again as the pressure increases.

1 The pump squeezes the freon under pressure.

PUMP

Jets and rockets

If you accidentally drop the hose-pipe while spraying the garden, you should grab it again quickly or run for cover. Instead of just lying there, the hose will wriggle and jump about squirting water in all directions. The hose-pipe is obeying one of the laws of physics. This law says that for every force there is an equal force pushing in the opposite direction. So, as water squirts from the hose, the nozzle tries to jump backwards in the opposite direction. The same thing happens when a hunter fires his gun. As the bullet shoots from the barrel, the gun jerks back against the hunter's shoulder. We call this force the 'recoil', and we use it in many machines, from garden sprinklers to jet engines.

Supersonic jet-power

The huge turbojet engines that power Concorde use exactly the same idea as the simple balloon jet shown above. Hot gases roar from the jet nozzles, and the recoil drives the aircraft forward through the air. The amount of recoil force (called thrust) that the engine can make depends on how much fuel it burns, and that depends on how much air it can suck in. So jet engines have big compressors at the front that force air into the engine at high pressure. Concorde can fly at twice the speed of sound.

Experiments with recoil

Does the recoil change if you use different-sized pebbles?

NAILS · PEBBLE · STRONG THREAD · RUBBER BAND · EMPTY TINS · MARKER · WOODEN BOARD

DRINKING STRAW · STICKY TAPE · PAPER ROLL OR PLASTIC TUBE · STRONG THREAD OR FISHING LINE

For safety, try this experiment out of doors. Set up a simple catapult gun like this, mounted on rollers, then fire it by cutting the thread. Watch what happens to the gun platform.

See how far you can fly a home-made balloon jet. The compressed air squirts from the jet nozzle and the recoil sends the balloon shooting along the guide line, just like a real jet engine.

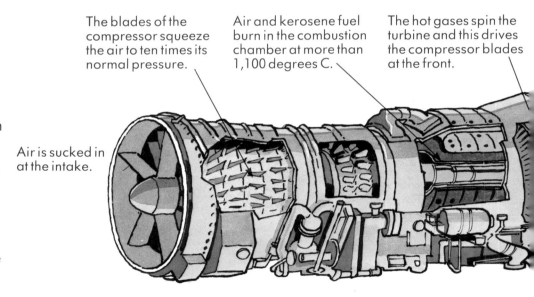

The blades of the compressor squeeze the air to ten times its normal pressure.

Air and kerosene fuel burn in the combustion chamber at more than 1,100 degrees C.

The hot gases spin the turbine and this drives the compressor blades at the front.

Air is sucked in at the intake.

All this talk about jets should help you explain why the sprinkler spins round without a motor.

One-mile land-speed record

In October 1983, an Englishman called Richard Noble drove his jet-powered car, Thrust 2, across the mud-flats of Black-rock Desert in America at 1,019.4kph (633.5mph). It was a new one-mile land-speed record.

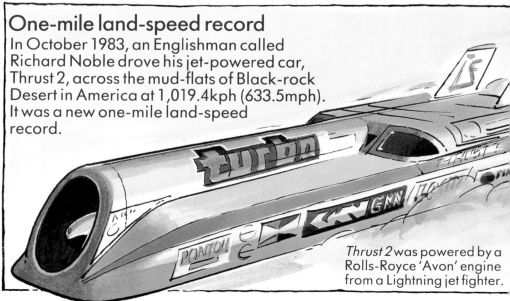

Thrust 2 was powered by a Rolls-Royce 'Avon' engine from a Lightning jet fighter.

You can make a steam-powered jet boat from a metal cigar tube or tablet tube. But candles and hot water can be dangerous, so take great care and ask a grown-up to help with the experiment.

METAL TUBE

SCREW CAP

CANDLE

SMALL HOLE MADE WITH A THIN NAIL

WIRE SUPPORTS

STEAM JET

PUT 2-3 TEASPOONS OF WATER INSIDE THE TUBE

BALSA WOOD BOAT

The gases are then forced out through the jet nozzle to produce the engine's powerful thrust.

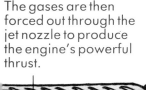

The car had a smooth aluminium skin to reduce the drag caused by friction with the air.

Next stop — the Moon

The Saturn V launch vehicle that carried American astronauts to the Moon was more than 110m tall and weighed as much as a loaded 70-truck goods train.

The huge first-stage rocket contained more than 2,000 tons of fuel, but it burned for only 2½ minutes before the second-stage rocket took over. By the time the third-stage rocket had burned out, the astronauts' capsule was hurtling through space at 11km a second.

Nothing can burn without oxygen, and as there is no oxygen beyond the Earth's atmosphere, space rockets have to carry their own supply. Without it they could not burn their rocket fuel. That is why nearly all the room inside the huge Saturn launch vehicle is taken up by tanks of fuel and liquid oxygen.

Who needs a runway?

The jet nozzles of the Harrier's engines can swivel to change the direction of thrust. By pointing them straight down, the aircraft can take off and land vertically. Once in the air, the nozzles are swivelled to point backwards and the Harrier can roar away in normal level flight.

Level flight

Thrust backwards

Aerofoil wings provide the aircraft's lift

Take-off and landing

Thrust downwards

Recoil provides the aircraft's lift

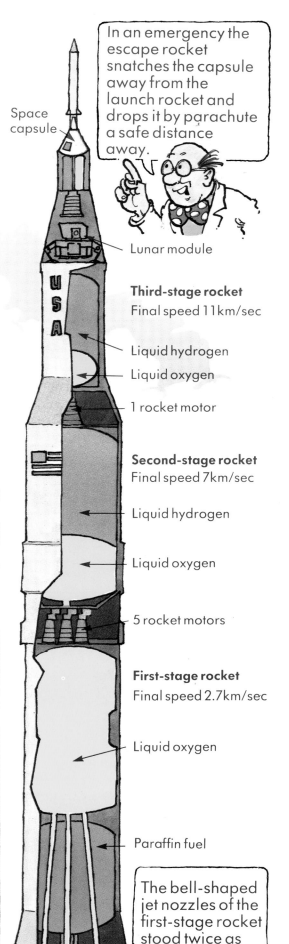

In an emergency the escape rocket snatches the capsule away from the launch rocket and drops it by parachute a safe distance away.

Space capsule

Lunar module

Third-stage rocket
Final speed 11km/sec

Liquid hydrogen

Liquid oxygen

1 rocket motor

Second-stage rocket
Final speed 7km/sec

Liquid hydrogen

Liquid oxygen

5 rocket motors

First-stage rocket
Final speed 2.7km/sec

Liquid oxygen

Paraffin fuel

The bell-shaped jet nozzles of the first-stage rocket stood twice as high as a man.

5 rocket motors

Stabilizing fins

115

The helicopter rotor

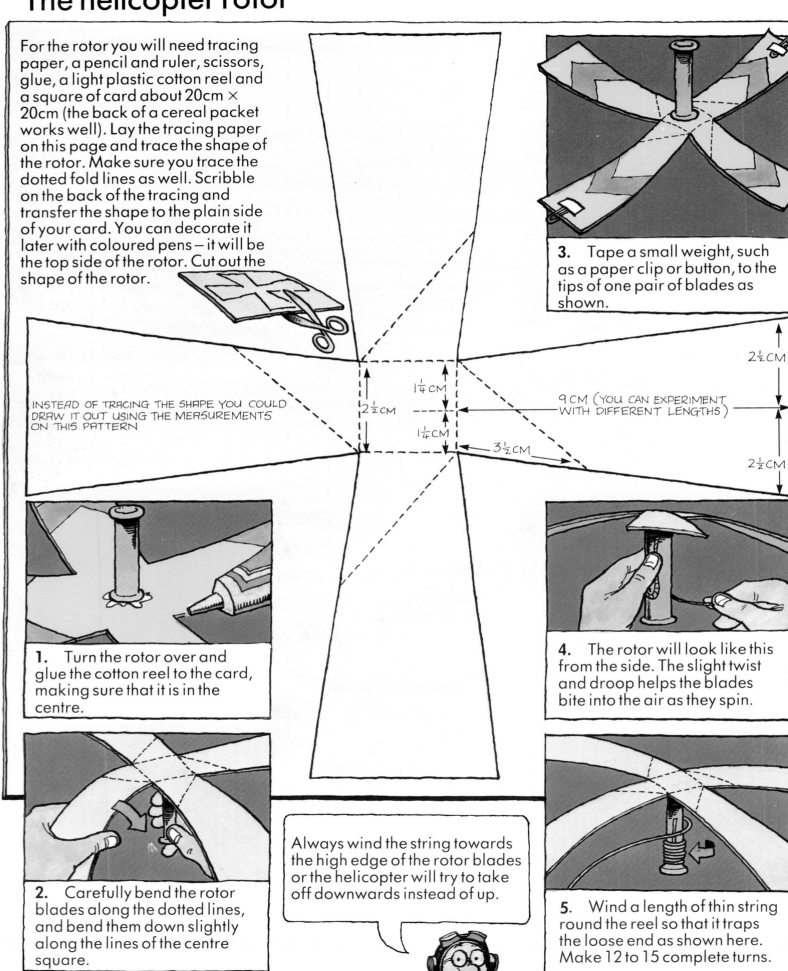

For the rotor you will need tracing paper, a pencil and ruler, scissors, glue, a light plastic cotton reel and a square of card about 20cm × 20cm (the back of a cereal packet works well). Lay the tracing paper on this page and trace the shape of the rotor. Make sure you trace the dotted fold lines as well. Scribble on the back of the tracing and transfer the shape to the plain side of your card. You can decorate it later with coloured pens – it will be the top side of the rotor. Cut out the shape of the rotor.

INSTEAD OF TRACING THE SHAPE YOU COULD DRAW IT OUT USING THE MEASUREMENTS ON THIS PATTERN

$2\frac{1}{2}$CM

$1\frac{1}{4}$CM

$1\frac{1}{4}$CM

$3\frac{1}{2}$CM

9 CM (YOU CAN EXPERIMENT WITH DIFFERENT LENGTHS)

$2\frac{1}{2}$CM

$2\frac{1}{2}$CM

3. Tape a small weight, such as a paper clip or button, to the tips of one pair of blades as shown.

1. Turn the rotor over and glue the cotton reel to the card, making sure that it is in the centre.

4. The rotor will look like this from the side. The slight twist and droop helps the blades bite into the air as they spin.

2. Carefully bend the rotor blades along the dotted lines, and bend them down slightly along the lines of the centre square.

Always wind the string towards the high edge of the rotor blades or the helicopter will try to take off downwards instead of up.

5. Wind a length of thin string round the reel so that it traps the loose end as shown here. Make 12 to 15 complete turns.

The hot air balloon

You will need a pencil and ruler, a stapler, glue, some newspaper, and twelve standard sheets of tissue paper joined in pairs along the short side to give six sheets roughly 50cm wide and 140cm long.

Fold the sheets in half so that the long edges meet. Then stack the folded sheets in a pile and staple the unfolded edges as shown.

Draw lines 5cm apart along and across the top sheet in the stack. Use this grid to copy the shape on the 1-cm grid opposite. Cut out the shape, cutting through all the sheets together.

Put some newspaper inside the first folded panel, then run a thin line of glue along the edge of the tissue paper. Place the next panel on top and press down along the edge.

Place newspaper inside the next panel, to stop any glue soaking through, then glue and position the next panel. Repeat until all six sheets are joined together.

This is the tricky bit. When the glue is dry, open up the concertina folds and glue the last two edges together to complete the balloon.

Finally, use a hair drier to blow up the balloon. This will not make it fly but it helps the glue dry and gives the balloon its proper shape, ready for the big launch.

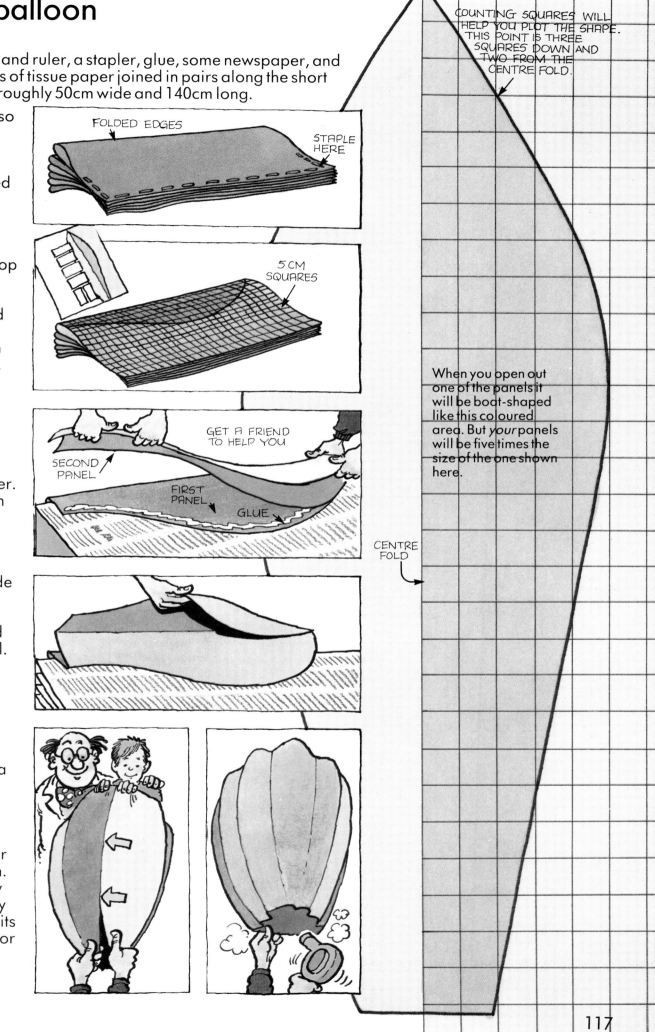

FOLDED EDGES

STAPLE HERE

5 CM SQUARES

GET A FRIEND TO HELP YOU

SECOND PANEL

FIRST PANEL

GLUE

COUNTING SQUARES WILL HELP YOU PLOT THE SHAPE. THIS POINT IS THREE SQUARES DOWN AND TWO FROM THE CENTRE FOLD.

When you open out one of the panels it will be boat-shaped like this coloured area. But *your* panels will be five times the size of the one shown here.

CENTRE FOLD

117

How Things Work Quiz

Questions

1 Is gravity on the Moon stronger or weaker than on Earth?

2 Which will fall over more easily; a bookcase with all the books on the top shelf or a bookcase with all the books on the bottom shelf?

3 Which of these sentences is true?
The longer the lever, the easier it is to lift something.
The shorter the lever, the easier it is to lift something.

4 Which takes more force; lifting a toy car straight up from the floor, or pulling it up a slope?

5 Do cranes use gears, screws or pulleys to lift heavy objects?

6 Which cause less friction; smooth surfaces or rough surfaces?

7 Why don't the loop-the-loop cars on a fairground ride fall off the track when they are upside-down?

8 If you have one gear with 12 teeth, linked to a smaller gear with 6 teeth, how many full turns will the smaller gear have made when the larger gear has made one full turn; 2, 6 or 12?

9 Do windmills need to have their sails facing the wind or away from the wind?

10 What is a meteorologist? Is it someone who studies rocks, meteors or the weather?

11 Is squashed air called thin air, compressed air or depressed air?

12 Do hydraulic machines use air, pulleys or liquids to push their pistons?

13 The American Rocket broke the world land-speed record in 1906. How was it powered?

14 Does metal expand or contract when it is heated?

15 What is the name for the amount of recoil force an engine can make; thrust, speed or compression?

Answers

1 The Moon's gravity is much weaker than the Earth's. See page 87.

2 A bookcase with all the books on the top shelf will fall over more easily than one with all the books on the bottom shelf because it has a higher centre of gravity. See page 89.

3 The longer the lever, the easier it is to lift something. See page 90.

4 Lifting a toy car straight up from the floor takes more force than pulling it up a slope. See page 92.

5 Cranes use pulleys to lift heavy objects. See page 95.

6 Smooth surfaces cause less friction than rough surfaces because things are more able to slide across them. See page 97.

7 Loop-the-loop cars stay on the track when they are upside-down because the outward force of the whirling cars presses them against the track. See page 98.

8 The smaller gear makes 2 turns for every full turn of the larger gear. See page 100.

9 Windmills need to have their sails facing the wind. See page 102.

10 A meteorologist is someone who studies the weather. (Someone who studies rocks is called a geologist and someone who studies meteors and other objects in space is an astronomer.) See page 105.

11 Squashed air is called compressed air. (There is no such thing as thin air or depressed air.) See page 104.

12 Hydraulic machines use liquids to push their pistons. See page 106.

13 The American car, Rocket, was powered by steam. See page 109.

14 Metal expands when heated, and contracts when cooled. See page 112.

15 The amount of recoil force an engine can make is called thrust. (Speed is how fast it can travel, and compression is when something is squeezed.) See page 114.

Index